SHOWCASE OF INTERIOR DESIGN

Pacific Edition II

Rockport/Vitae Publishing, Inc.

1997 Rockport/Vitae Publishing, Inc.
All rights reserved under International
and Pan-American Copyright Convention.
Published in the United States
by Rockport/Vitae Publishing, Inc.
146 Granite Street
Rockport, Massachusetts 01966
508-546-9590

Library of Congress
Cataloging-in-Publication Data

Showcase of Interior Design, Pacific Edition II
p. cm.
Includes indexes.
ISBN 1-883065-08-9 (hard)
1. Interior decoration—California—Pacific Coast—History—20th century
I. Crouch, Elizabeth
NK 2004.S55 1996 728' .09794'909049—DC20

ROCKPORT/VITAE PUBLISHING, INC.

CHAIRMAN - JOHN C. AVES
PRESIDENT - JAMES C. MARKLE

PACIFIC EDITION II PRODUCTION STAFF

Communication Manager - Christine H. Hoek
Communication Assistants - Alison Aves & Katrina V. Lefler
Production Manager - Brian Hudgens
Production Artist - Nancy J. Allen
Copy Editor - David Knorr
Financial Management - Lisa Remington
Client Services Manager - Carolyn Zank

REGIONAL EDITORS

Gail Hayes Adams, FASID
Pamela Blakeney
Gregory J. Dekker
John Inge
Judith K. Oppenheimer
Francine Port

Printed in China
Typeset in USA by Vitae Publishing, Inc.

Title page Interior Design: Casa Del Encanto
Photo: Tom Clark

TABLE
OF
CONTENTS

Consensus From The Pacific Coast: "In The World Of Interior Design Today, This Is The Nexus, The Hub."

A Conversation with Eight Showcase *Designers*
By Elizabeth Crouch

Above the roar of the surf, the hum of freeways and the sputter of cappuccino machines, the voices of interior designers working on the Pacific Coast today are rising on a warm wind of enthusiasm. Word is out around the world – everything is coming together here. And the rest of the world is listening.

A sea change in possibilities

When Thomas Achille came to Southern California from the East Coast 25 years ago, Los Angeles was a sleepy little town. "In the 70s it seemed like an outpost. Today it's the leading design market in the world – the Hong Kong, the New York, or Paris of the late 20s. We're surrounded by incredible tradespeople and artisans. If you need a *shoji* screen, there's someone down the block who will make one for you, or if you want hammered iron from Romania, there's a guy over there who's an expert. I can't think of any other place in the world where this can happen."

OPPOSITE: Edward C. Turrentine, ASID: A medley of arches and capitals combines with a collection of richly traditional furnishings to create a livable room fit for a museum.

Frank Pennino, looking up the coast from his offices in Los Angeles, tells us that between L.A. and San Francisco there is a wonderful cross-section of suppliers. This is especially important to him since he works with collections and period furniture, seeking out choice pieces from West Coast auctions and antique dealers. "People from all over the world are coming here to buy."

In the midst of this sea change in sources and possibilities, Carol Poet – like many designers established in Southern California – maintains her ties to the East Coast and respects the wonderful contemporary design it produces. But nothing escapes the West Coast for long. "I may see something in New York that I get excited about, come flying back and in a few weeks I'll see it in a showroom in California."

For Gary Gibson, the range of choices from San Diego and L.A. to Santa Barbara and San Francisco offers tremendous design possibilities. "I constantly get phone calls from people who say, 'I do these wonderfully unique things.' Even though you don't have need at the time, it may spark an idea you'll draw upon later."

"*Artisan* is the key word," says Carol Meltzer. "Today California is artisan. And there is tremendous respect for their work." Because of the quality and more reasonable cost of specialized workmanship in the region, it isn't unusual for Andy Gerhard to take his crew with him when he does projects in other parts of the country.

With so much at their doorstep, why would West Coast designers look anywhere else? Most often they don't. Ron Wilson still enjoys shopping in New York and Europe. "But that's why I do it – for the enjoyment, not because I can't find the right piece here."

It's a world market

Designers are also finding that when they want to extend their reach, as inevitably they do, they have easy access to sources around the world. "For the designer today," Pennino emphasizes, "it has become a world market. It used to be, for example, that you could find only three or four different kinds of plumbing fittings and everyone bought the same sort of thing. Now, with the advent of information technology, we know what they're doing in England or Germany or Italy. The average person simply doesn't have the time or the connections to access all of these sources."

For Craig Wright, occasional trips abroad still yield wonderful finds. But on the wings of electronics he can go shopping at auctions around the world. Typically, his weekends are spent poring over the five to ten catalogues he receives a day. "You go through them to find that little piece of silver, that Fabergé elephant saltcellar, or that piece of Flora Danica from Denmark. You can shop at your desk with these catalogues, and we have people around the world who bid for us. Of course, there's no one way to buy. You have to know your markets. Sometimes you can find something next door that's very inexpensive, or pay twice as much in an obscure village in Italy."

Everything isn't off-white and overstuffed

With the world shrinking and L.A. expanding, the ripples of influences have turned into waves. Gibson, a native, sees the influx of people from all over the world as having an enormous effect on the direction of interior design. "People are quick to think there's a 'California style,' but really that look – the neutral tones, sculptural furniture, the Zen, minimalist look – is something of the past. You may see it at the beach, but not in the Hollywood hills. While we have retained the natural colors and materials – the rich earth tones along with the wheat, beige and cream, as well as the raffia, rattan and sisal – we've broadened our horizons, adding more to the mix, enriching it to make it better."

Designers point out that in architecture as well as in furnishings and art, there is tremendous cultural diversity. "It's reflective of our universe," says Meltzer. "We are more of a mix – a *potpourri* – and that's the fun of it."

Poet, whose interest in design began with the fashion industry, has a sharp eye for changes in style. "What's so interesting about the times now is that everything goes – every style flies. In the past we've seen dark periods with very heavy woods, moving to very light woods and a whitewashed effect. That's not to say that there aren't still whitewashed rooms or dark-paneled walls. If they are done well, they still have longevity."

Gerhard also believes we've moved beyond some of the fleeting trends of the past – "the 50s with that awful avocado green and harvest gold, or the 60s with the turquoise and green together. That sort of thing just doesn't seem to be happening today."

Wilson sees a cyclical pattern to interior design on the West Coast. "Over the past 20 years, decoration has both evolved and turned around on itself. For example, over the past ten years or so, it was 'overstuffed and off-white.' The trend was a carefree, lighthearted, monotone interior, as if it would be there forever. But in the past couple of years," Wilson explains, "that look has begun to fade away. What has returned is traditional. Antique markets are extremely busy again. Deeper, darker, more luxurious fabrics are very appropriate. It's as if Southern California were a world all its own. We make tremendous changes here. And when we begin the change, most people follow."

The latest trend in clients

With the West Coast's growing diversity comes a new level of sophistication and education on the part of clients themselves. "They do their homework," observes Achille. "They are more knowledgeable about antiques and architecture, and they are conversant with Tuscan, Neoclassic, Italianate or Post Modern." He attributes this

BELOW: J. Powell & Associates,Inc.: Dark colors and uncluttered accessories strengthen the sophistication of this contemporary dining area.

knowledge to the vast array of magazines, books and marketing venues now available. "In the past it was more designer as teacher, now it's more designer as filter."

Among these more knowledgeable clients, designers note a definite shift. "We see our younger clients wanting to return to a more traditional style of architecture," says Pennino, who teaches architecture at UCLA. "They are looking for warmth, personality and a little bit of quirkiness. People today want a more relaxed living style, more forgiving to the dogs and the children – a little less hard-edged. They don't want to live in a home where everything on the cocktail table has to be in the right place, otherwise it ruins the composition." Pennino also believes that in new home construction the market wants a more traditional reflection. "These houses don't have to be slavish copies of the past. When Jefferson did Monticello, he took a classical style and made it more wonderful."

Traditional homes, while popular today, tend to be stirred up in new ways with lots of light and often a combination of contemporary and traditional furniture. "People are using their primary residence not so much for entertaining as for themselves," says Wright. "The dining room today is used for family dining and the drawing room is used as another room for the family. In the past, people retreated to the library or study. Now they want to get out of those little rooms and back to the large, light-filled spaces."

Enumerating the priorities of clients today, Meltzer believes that comfort tops the list, followed by a feeling of safety and also a sense of tradition. "Tradition is very important: as we keep mixing, our homes will mirror that mix. The client is also more in alignment with nature – the gardens on the exterior are more visible." She sees a movement away from the formal, toward making the house respond to the way people want to live. "People are building libraries into their kitchens, and houses are becoming more child-friendly. Even in the older homes you incorporate the media room, and of course everyone wants a home office."

Gerhard also sees much more attention to conveniences. "People today are more interested in their bathrooms and kitchens – making things functional. That to me is the biggest change. Twenty-five years ago, clients would give some thought to closets, but not like today. Now closets are extremely important. And many of my clients want the advantage of the latest mechanics. At the push of a button, they can have TVs coming out of the floors, walls or ceiling." When asked if greater functionality dictates a more informal approach, Gerhard responds with an emphatic, "No, it does not." He explains: "If you're a designer, not a decorator, you can achieve a formal feel in a home and still the rooms can be very comfortable and enjoyable as well as functional."

Achille, who touts L.A. as a remarkable city, is quick to point out that because of its size and density, "people are more apt to want to close themselves off, to insulate themselves. They're into taking second homes where they can get away. I have clients for whom I'm doing boats and yachts. More and more people are looking for a retreat from the stressful aspects of daily life in a big city."

Not wanting to leave

Comfort tops the list of what clients and designers try to bring to the home. A level of comfort is also what both parties need to establish with one another. In testing a relationship, most designers visit the client's home to see what they have, what they love, or what they collect. Poet describes it as a two-way interview process. "After having a cup of coffee together and talking in general terms, you know fairly quickly whether you want to spend a lot of time together and whether you are on the same wavelength."

"Often clients will come to me with a photo they've torn out of a magazine and have been saving for years," says Gerhard. "It's something they like, but frequently they don't know why. After a few meetings, you are able to understand what attracted them and you can build on that."

Achille tries to anticipate how a client's interests may develop. "Today they love Spanish furniture, but they also show interest in English. In five years their love of English may grow. It's important to take time, to try to recognize where a client is headed." For Meltzer, interior design is also the art of observation. "First you see what's important, what people want to present to other people; then you notice what makes them comfortable, how they relax, how they want their space to work."

For Wright, the process begins with the house. "The house tells you certain things and you pay attention to the architecture." He believes that rooms don't have to be large or overly furnished. "They have to be interesting – have a catch to them. You don't want rooms that are too obvious in the beginning. You want to be able to discover layers."

Much of Pennino's work is influenced by his clients' collections – perhaps fine Indian art or Americana. "Clients come to me and say: 'We love this house, this is our collection, and this is the kind of furniture we feel comfortable with.' Then the issue is, how can we create an environment that brings

OPPOSITE: Sistine Interiors: Timeless accessories bring a serene quality to a setting that celebrates the natural environment.

together all of these elements. It's really a conversation between the house, the client and myself."

While most designers visit the client's home, Wilson opens the door the other way, suggesting that clients come to him. "When clients walk into a project of mine, it's not important whether they like French versus contemporary furniture. But no matter what design they're observing, if they don't feel immediately comfortable in a room, I believe it's the wrong relationship. It's not the 'Oh my God, isn't this beautiful' I'm looking for. It's having that person sit down and not want to leave. That's when I say – 'This is it.'"

It's a big mix, but it isn't easy

"Today people want to broaden their horizons and stir things up," says Wright. "But it's always dangerous to throw out the rules. Novices can say, 'Oh well, we can do that. It's just a big mix.' They go to the flea markets, throw it all together and come out with absolutely nothing. About half of the jobs that come to me involve people who try to do it on their own and run into trouble. They say, 'Why didn't I come to you sooner?' Often, if people would go to a professional at the beginning, they would spend half the money."

Meltzer agrees that because there are no rules, interior design today requires more knowledge. She too is called upon to rescue people for whom do-it-yourself has reached crisis proportions. "In the area of lighting, for example, you need a professional. You can't light up a whole home at night with halogen, although when it comes to what people will try, you'd be surprised! Lighting can make a room welcoming or make someone want to leave very fast."

With the tremendous advances in lighting and mechanics available today, Gerhard wants to be able to pull out all the stops, but without letting these innovations dominate. "You don't want to walk into the room and have the lighting say – 'Look at me!' Sure, you want all the mechanics you can possibly have, but you also want to keep it subtle."

And then there is color. Gibson, who believes that strong color doesn't have to be jarring, often mixes it on the spot. "I did a Santa Fe house with red walls, using layers of color. You have to educate your clients as you go along, showing them how you achieve the right balance in values and hues. Color is wonderful because it changes the feeling and creates a mood, but you have to know what you're doing."

Beyond the demands of aesthetics, the complexity of homes today makes the designer even more indispensable than in the past. Gibson suggests these analogies: "It's as if you're the art director, or you're putting together a big jigsaw puzzle. You have to work well with the architect, the builder, the subs – it's a team." And the designer heads that team, bringing together every facet of the project. Meltzer describes a typical scenario: "The electrician is there pulling his wires, and I'm trying to tie in the computer guy, the lighting guy and the sound guy. Yes, it's a challenge...but it's fun, because we're moving into a whole new era. As a designer, I have to equip homes so they will work not just for today, but for the future."

The art of collaboration

Most designers see their projects as collaborations. "You have to build a trust, you are becoming one – a unit," says

Gibson. "If you're building a house, you may be working on it for a year or more, and everyone has to get along."

Wright is finding that today's clients are eager to be involved. Like other *Showcase* designers, he welcomes their input. "They want to play a part in finding that painting from the Onassis sale, or incorporating a piece they've found in their travels – something with their own imprint. You want to create a background where things can be added without destroying the whole composition."

"Because there are so many styles to choose from and so many resources available," observes Poet, "it can get a little confusing for the client. In fact, I've had calls from other designers who tell me they're doing their own homes and are completely stuck. They'll say, 'Please come over and help!' So you see, even the designer benefits from collaboration."

And collaboration can take many forms – abbreviated or extended. Wright tells of a project he did for a well-known contemporary architect. "I met with his wife for 20 minutes. She gave me an overview – a very carefully collected group of photographs. Nothing specific, only the spirit. We worked for two years on the house. When she came to see it she said: 'It's our best possession.' Then there are the clients whose house we have worked on for 18 years. As they have grown, the house has grown, becoming better and better."

Sometimes the requirements of the client are sweeping. For Poet, there was the client who said: "Let's base the house entirely on earthy elements." She tapped into every resource imaginable, pulling together elements of bronze, copper, silver, and stone – even cement with

OPPOSITE: C. M. Wright, Inc.: Note how the palm tree and blue door frames add splashes of color to a living space that relies on simple, comfortable white furnishings.

its warm, silver base. In other situations, the client's requirement can be modest, verging on humble. Wright recalls doing an enormous limestone house for a couple. "The husband's only request was to have a little table to put his briefcase on when he came home from work. Of course, every situation is different. It's wonderful when both husband and wife agree. But when they don't, often you can satisfy their needs in different rooms – 'Here you get your lavender curtains, there you get your marble.'"

Accomplished designers aren't afraid to admit they learn from their clients. Wilson, who has been working with Cher for 25 years tells us: "She forces me to go beyond myself and never wants to repeat what we've done before. After 17 projects, it's not easy to come up with yet another idea. She remembers the last little piece of gimp that was used three houses ago."

What the designer brings to the table

Increasingly, designers are expediting the process of new construction as well as adaptation projects by working up front with architects. "It used to be poison for architects to hear that interior designers were involved," says Wilson. "That has changed dramatically." Gerhard agrees: "Collaborating with the architect from the beginning is the best thing that can happen on a project. We put our egos aside, and go to work for the client."

Wright believes there are many areas of architectural planning which can benefit from the designer's input. "Building standards for mainstream America aren't necessarily what a more affluent client needs. Specifying kitchen cabinets to a standard depth may not accommodate our client's service plates. And with closets as well there can be some fatal mistakes – not allowing enough room for gowns and padded shoulders, or not providing enough light."

The designer is also the checkpoint for practicality. Gibson has no qualms about warning clients if something isn't appropriate. "After all, they're paying me to help them. I'll tell them: 'You have five dogs and you want white Berber carpet. You're crazy.' But, you also have to know the art of compromise."

Because of the cultural diversity in our society today, designers must be attuned to many traditions. Meltzer, who deals with many Asian clients, has herself become a licensed practitioner of *Feng Shui* – the Far Eastern art of laying out structures. For clients concerned with placing the computer in the "prosperity zone," specialized training enables her to comply.

Designers are full of surprises. They can bring to the project features a client could never produce on his own, sometimes creating custom pieces. Recently, Poet designed a very comfortable but compact chair and ottoman covered in boar hide to fill the specific need of a small space. "Then I located a wonderful *atelier* where we could have it made."

Gerhard often designs carpet for his projects to compliment the architecture. Or when a space requires original art, he will have a piece commissioned. "It's wonderful to take an artist to a project and say, 'Here is the space, come to me with a concept.' Giving an artist this freedom usually results in the best work."

The experienced designer honors the interests of the individual, but takes those interests to a new level. "We try to give clients something they will grow into," says Pennino. "If they want pine furniture, we want to introduce them to Georgian pine; if they want mahogany, we want them to consider 18th-century mahogany." Poet would agree. "If it's a good purchase – if it's a good piece to begin with – it won't go out of style."

When rooms are done well, they have lasting value. Gerhard recently revisited a project in Iowa he had completed in 1979. After so many years, he expected the interior might look out of date. But he was pleasantly surprised. "The only thing I would have changed were the throw pillows which, by today's standards, were rather small. Everything else seemed as right as before."

A feeling without words

Each designer seems to look at his work through a different lens. "I approach it all as art," says Gibson, an accomplished artist himself. "I may take as my starting point a tile in the house. If an element has intrinsic value, it can provide the basis for an entire color scheme."

Poet's early experience in the fashion industry makes her highly sensitive to textiles and the weave of fabrics. She brings samples to her clients so that they can feel the textures. "Fabrics," as she puts it, "should have a 'good hand.'"

For Meltzer, working with Japan and other parts of Asia has brought a refined perspective. "Far Eastern designers are very pure, open and fresh. They work with the balance of less is more. I think some of this influence has mellowed California. New Yorkers used to say about Californians, 'They're so garish;' and Californians about New Yorkers, 'They're so traditional, up tight.' But people are becoming more bi-coastal, exchanging their views. So in California today you see a bit of toning down."

Pennino's scholarly background in architecture enables

him to work on houses requiring restoration as well as furnishing. While he likes to keep a unified time frame in his projects, he is not tied to any one period. "I'm as partial to Italian and French furniture as to English. I love very good Art Deco as much as fine 18th-century French."

Gerhard is very particular about the background – wall treatments, ceilings and flooring. "I like for things to flow, to enhance the architecture of the house. We're very particular with these elements, and this is where we shine. We love doing moldings and working with the architect on window details, pockets for draperies and also the lighting which is so important. As a firm, we don't have a definite look: we go from knife-edge contemporary to Louis XVI traditional."

BELOW: Gerhard Design Group: Exterior and interior design merge through a wall of windows in this uniquely enchanting master bedroom.

Achille's creative exuberance thrives in the expansive design mood of the West Coast today. "While you can do better traditional here than any place else, you're not bound to traditional. Clients allow you a great deal of freedom. You can take chances with scale, color and light. You get quite remarkable style – very worldly."

"The feeling – something that is without words" is the way Wilson describes that all-important quality he, the designer, tries to bring to a project. "A client can go to a furniture store and say: 'I'll have that room and that room.' But there's something missing. To me, it doesn't matter what the individual likes of the client might be – all French or all Japanese. But it had better be serious French or Japanese. There's no style I wouldn't enjoy doing, so long as it's real."

Wright, who delights in visual counterpoint, uses antiques "to provide a sense of warmth and age." He also enjoys exotic combinations – very simple upholstery with extravagant pillows and tapestries. In a study he is designing for a producer, he has used a leather floor and, for a rug, a Brussels tapestry with enormous horses and warring Romans.

"I'm leaving, they're staying"

For Achille, ultimately interior design is about service. "In getting to understand their needs, clients come to depend on us. If they don't like the way the door closes on the closet, they pick up the phone and call us. They think we're a fountain of knowledge. I've had clients come to me and ask: 'Who makes the best wedding cakes in L.A.?' Or, 'Where do you stay in Paris?'"

Poet has clients who disappear for months on location.

"They tell me, 'We're coming back on a certain day, and we're going to have a dinner party that night.'" She suspects that these pressures account for interior designers' being in the same insurance category for stress as air-traffic controllers. "You really are at the nexus of so many things that must come together and can't collide."

Meltzer believes that the interior designer opens up an awareness – helps people to find themselves. "It's about the individual – what's right for them, not what's right for me. I tell myself: 'I'm leaving, but they're staying.'"

Like other *Showcase* designers, Wright enjoys working with people who want to have fun with their homes. "They're the clients you will jump through hoops for – the ones who want to expand their horizons. As a result, they get the best projects."

"Oh, I never would have thought of that!" is the expression Gibson most likes to hear from a client. He speaks for all of our designers when he says, "The process should be fun. Of course there's Murphy's law – things will go wrong. But it can all be corrected. And in the final analysis, those things really make the project more fun. Once you've found the designer who's right for you, just enjoy it. You'll have a wonderful time."

Elizabeth Crouch is a contributing writer to Vitae Publishing and to Aves Inc. Formerly, she was Associate and Acting Director of The Grand Rapids Art Museum in Grand Rapids, Michigan, and Acting Director of The Mint Museum of Art in Charlotte, North Carolina. During the Kennedy and Johnson Administrations, she served as Registrar of Art at The White House.

THOMAS C. ACHILLE AND ASSOCIATES, INTERIOR DESIGN

THOMAS C. ACHILLE
521 NORTH LA CIENEGA BLVD., SUITE 10
LOS ANGELES, CA 90048
(310)659-0300   FAX (310)659-7981

PROJECTS:
Private Residences: Homes and estates throughout California including Beverly Hills, Bel Air, Brentwood, Santa Monica, Hancock Park, Portola Valley, Palo Alto, and the Monterey Peninsula. East Coast projects include New York City and Georgetown, Washington D.C.

Commercial Work: Beverly Hills and Los Angeles.

PUBLISHED IN:
Architectural Digest

PHILOSOPHY:
A timeless blend of classic and contemporary elements, related to the client's own personal style is the hallmark of Thomas C. Achille & Associates.

BELOW: The classic lines of the background are a perfect foil for the mix of contemporary and traditional furniture.

OPPOSITE: A grand entrance hall in a home designed by architect Paul Williams. The complete restoration of this home was accomplished in a two year period. The warm, stately elegance of this two story entrance hall sets the tone for the rest of the house and gardens.

Thomas C. Achille And Associates, Interior Design

RIGHT: Warm wood tones on the antique Biedermeier game table and inlaid veneers on the antique French commode balance the gilt wood and golden yellow colors in this Morning Room.

BELOW: Venetian red upholstery blends with a gilt empire chandelier and gilt wood accessories, while cobalt blue highlights and a mirrored wall bring the room magically alive.

OPPOSITE: A conservatory done in shades of peach, celadon and creme. The silk fabrics and chinoiserie furnishings create an ethereal vision crowned by Romanesque trompe l'oeil clouds on the ceiling.

GAIL ADAMS
INTERIORS LTD.

GAIL HAYES ADAMS, FASID
110 EAST SAN MIGUEL
PHOENIX, AZ 85012
(602) 274-0074 FAX (602) 274-8897

1820 AVENIDA DEL MUNDO
CORONADO, CA 92118
(619) 435-8268

PROJECTS:
Private Residences: Arizona, California, Colorado and Michigan.

Commercial Work: Health care facilities, hospitality facilities and executive offices.

CREDENTIALS:
Who's Who in Interior Design
ASID, National President, 1985
Fellow of ASID
Who's Who in America

PUBLISHED IN:
The Designer
Designers West
Phoenix Home & Garden
Phoenix Magazine
Arizona Business & Development
Southwest Passages

LEFT: The custom-designed table and chairs play off the fabric on the seat pads. A blue arch frames the breakfast area and adds a degree of intensity.

BELOW: Family antiques and warm colors create a cozy environment for fine and casual dining.

OPPOSITE: Stones found on the homeowner's property inspired the color palette in this comfortable space.

GAIL ADAMS
INTERIORS LTD.

PHILOSOPHY:
I am dedicated to creating comfortable, distinctive and enduring interiors that reflect the lifestyle and objectives of my clients. To ensure client satisfaction, I personally oversee all phases of design in every residential and commercial project.

RIGHT: Inviting textures and soft colors come together in a relaxing master bedroom.

BELOW: Designed for a professional football player, this casual media room features a custom video cabinet with room for showcasing helmets from current and former teams.

ABOVE OPPOSITE: Artwork and fabrics in this contemporary living room rely on the rich palette of the Southwest.

BELOW OPPOSITE: Vibrant, rich colors provide a beautiful contrast to a contemporary, neutral background.

PAULA BERG
DESIGN
ASSOCIATES, INC.

PAULA BERG
7522 EAST MCDONALD
SCOTTSDALE, AZ 85251
(602)998-2344   FAX: (602)951-0165

PROJECTS:
Private Residences: Aspen and Vail, Colorado; Carefree, Paradise Valley, Phoenix, Scottsdale and Tucson, Arizona; Deer Valley, Utah; Orlando, Miami and Tampa, Florida; Seattle; Dallas; Taos and Santa Fe, New Mexico; Los Angeles; San Diego; Atlanta; and Boston.

Commercial Work: Model homes in San Diego and Phoenix; offices, restaurants and retail stores.

LEFT: This contemporary Southwest desert home reflects the designer's passion for using texture and natural elements to create an earthy feel.

BELOW: Richly textured overscaled chairs, a contemporary interpretation of a tribal rug, and a fireplace covered in patina metal blend in warm harmony in this mountain retreat.

OPPOSITE: A blend of contemporary furnishings is juxtaposed against a rugged stone fireplace in this eclectic design.

PAULA BERG
DESIGN
ASSOCIATES, INC.

CREDENTIALS:
ASID, Allied Member
Ohio University, B.S. Communications
Georgia State University School of
 Fine Arts – Graduate program
Who's Who in Interior Design,
 1994-1995
Lecturer for Phoenix Home & Garden
 Seminars
Street of Dreams, Best Interior Design,
 1988
Heard Museum Designers' Showhouse,
 1989
Phoenix Home & Garden Designers'
 Showhouse, 1991
Phoenix Home & Garden "Masters
 of the Southwest"
Southwest Passages Showhouse, 1992
Southwest Passages Showhouse, 1993
Multiple ASID Excellence in Design
 Awards, 1992
Multiple ASID Excellence in Design
 Awards, 1993 (including a sweep
 of product design)

PUBLISHED IN:
Home
Interior Designers Showcase of Color
Phoenix Home & Garden
Phoenix Magazine
San Diego Home & Garden
Southwest Expressions
Southwest Passages
West

PHILOSOPHY:
My goal is to create environments
that work in harmony with the changing
lifestyle and personality of my clients.
Quality detailing, unique finishes and
comfortable textures are the foundation
of my approach to design, while the
use of natural elements gives my
interiors a sense of earthiness.

*ABOVE RIGHT: Southwest goes
uptown in this sophisticated
game room. Using a rich mix of
maple and cherry with ebony
accents, Paula Berg created a
contemporary adaptation of
Biedermeier style.*

*BELOW: Touches of gold and
bronze accent neutral beiges
and blacks, lending a sense of
quiet opulence to this master
suite.*

*OPPOSITE: Melding the
richness of Old World style
with contemporary elegance,
this anteroom to a carriage
house was featured in the 1993
Southwest Passages Showhouse.
Acid-etched concrete floors were
introduced to the Phoenix area
through this project, which won
an ASID first-place award.*

KIMBERLY BRAGG
INTERIOR DESIGN

KIMBERLY BRAGG
3364 SACRAMENTO ST.
SAN FRANCISCO, CA 94118
(415)563-8122   FAX (415)567-7374

PROJECTS:
Private Residences: San Francisco; New York; La Jolla, California; Oregon; and London.

Commercial Work: Corporate offices, restaurants and hospitals.

PUBLICATIONS:
Northern California Home & Garden
Diablo Magazine
San Francisco Chronicle
Sacramento Bee
House & Garden
Sunset Books
C'est Ya (Japan)

PHILOSOPHY:
   Good design is based on proper use of scale, color and proportion. More important, good design means listening to clients and keeping an open dialogue that encourages collaboration. The results should be magical.

CANNON/BULLOCK

RICHARD A. CANNON, IIDA
RICHARD P. BULLOCK, ASSOC. IIDA
9903 SANTA MONICA BOULEVARD
SUITE 605
BEVERLY HILLS, CA 90212

STUDIO at THE BREWERY
612 MOULTON AVENUE, STUDIO #4
LOS ANGELES, CA 90031

(213)221-9286

BELOW: A large studio/gallery space where actor Tony Curtis entertains and displays his artwork is divided into "rooms" with rugs and drapery.

BOTTOM: One thousand yards of fabric create giant tents masking unsightly ceilings in a nightclub/restaurant recalling Hollywood's famous Coconut Grove.

OPPOSITE: One wall is gold leafed and another is stenciled with tiny falling leaves to effect an aura of shimmering romance in candlelight.

PROJECTS:
Private Residences: United States and Canada.

Commercial Work: Restaurants and nightclubs, law and executive offices, retail shops, showrooms, and exhibit and museum buildings. Design products in showrooms nationwide.

ABOVE LEFT: Lush cushions and pillows complement a hand-marbleized silk drapery in this restful reading nook.

ABOVE RIGHT: Color, pattern and a trompe l'oeil niche bring a dark alcove to life.

LEFT: Bed drapery panels suggest a cozier "room within a room" in a large, open studio divided with partitions and drapery to create more intimate spaces.

ABOVE OPPOSITE: Wall upholstery, deep warm colors and antiques give this guest room a memorable European feeling.

BELOW OPPOSITE: Stenciling, faux tortoise shell crown mouldings and strong color add traditional grace to a "Monterey Colonial" in San Marino.

PHILOSOPHY:
A love of color, a sense of humor, a respect for tradition and the "bones" of good architecture underlie our approach to design.
  Within the context of function, we make dramatic, memorable spaces that whisper "remember me" into your ear long after you have departed.

CREDENTIALS:
California State Polytechnic University, B. Arch.
Wesleyan University, B.A.
University of Hawaii
Universita De Firenze/Internationals Program
Oxford University, England
Portland Museum Art School
IIDA, Member
California Certified Interior Designer, #3407
Royal Architectural Institute of Canada
Lecturer:
  University of British Columbia
  California Polytechnic University
  University of Washington
  Portland State University
  Art Center College of Design

CAROL TOLKAN
DESIGNS

CAROL TOLKAN KIESCHNICK
1089 GREEN VALLEY ROAD
NAPA, CA 94558
(707)224-8392   FAX (707)224-8393

5317 COLDWATER CYN AVENUE, UNIT A
SHERMAN OAKS, CA 91401
(818)981-7751   FAX (818)981-7753

RIGHT: Cantaloupe and rose fabric in a modified chevron pattern provides a dose of subdued color in an otherwise neutral master bedroom.

BELOW: Artful space planning allows a large, open room to serve several functions.

PROJECTS:
Private Residences: California and
Colorado.

Commercial Work: Children's Social
Services, University of Southern
California; Pasadena Showcase House;
Little Company of Mary, Palos Verdes,
California; Sand Pipers, Palos Verdes,
California; lodges, hotels, condominiums
and restaurants, Aspen, Colorado;
Toyota dealerships, Cathedral City and
Duarte, California.

CREDENTIALS:
ASID, Professional Member
AIA & AIF, Associate Member
NARI
CCICD
Woodbury College
UCLA School of Interior Design
LA Trade Tech, fashion design degree

*BELOW: Stark contrast
between black, white and gold
is the foremost characteristic
in an interior that uses floral
arrangements as its accent
color.*

CASA DEL ENCANTO

LUIS CORONA
6939 E. 1ST. AVE.
SCOTTSDALE, AZ 85251
(602)266-7755   FAX (602)266-5251

MICHAEL BARRON

PROJECTS:
Private Residences: Sedona, Chandler, Glendale, Phoenix, Scottsdale, Paradise Valley, Pinnacle Peak, Carefree and Ahwatukee, Arizona; and San Diego.

Commercial Work: Numerous projects in Phoenix and Tucson, including law offices, restaurants, Cathy's Rum Cake and Raven Golf Courses.

CREDENTIALS:
ASID First Place
1994 Design Excellence
Offices under 10,000 square feet

ASID First Place
1994 Design Excellence
Showcase Houses

ASID First Place
1994 Design Excellence
Singular Space

ASID Second Place
1995 Design Excellence
Hospitality

ASID Second Place
1993 Excellence in Design
Residential over 3,000 square feet

ASID Third Place
1992 Excellence in Design
Offices under 10,000 square feet

PUBLISHED IN:
Southwest Passages
Phoenix Magazine
Phoenix Home and Garden
Sunset Magazine
Arizona Style
Arizona Business Journal
Destination Arizona

PHILOSOPHY:
Our philosophy is simple. We design for our client's ego, not ours.
  We try to incorporate the outdoors into our space through the use of natural materials, wood, stone, metal and glass. Our interior and exterior architectural detailing creates enchanted homes that emphasize the understated luxury sought by our clients.

THIS PAGE: Custom Paradisio granite floors and countertops update this 1950s St. Charles kitchen with a dramatic, classic look. Recessed halogen lighting, matte amburgine lacquer walls and crisp white lacquer wainscotting complete the project.

OPPOSITE: Against a canvas of neutral tones and lustrous cherry floors, the textures and colors of chenilles, tapestries and jewel-toned accents add flavor to a comfortable living area.

CASA DEL ENCANTO

These two small rooms in the 1994 Southwest Passages Designers Show House *presented a number of logistical challenges, including the absence of natural light.*

RIGHT: Stone carved columns with a grape design add architectural interest to the corners and carry the grapevine theme throughout the parlor.

BELOW: In this melting pot of Old World craftsmanship, a painting of an archangel hangs above an old Italian carpenter's bench, which serves as a console. The harvest table and church benches, dating from the 1600s, are from Mexico.

OPPOSITE: The walls and ceiling are constructed of stone blocks in the wine sitting area. The softly lit niches house authentic religious art commonly known as "Retablos."

MICHAEL C.F. CHAN & ASSOCIATES, INC.

MICHAEL C.F. CHAN, AIA
3550 W. 6TH ST., PENTHOUSE
LOS ANGELES, CA 90020
(213)383-2162   FAX (213)383-1815

PROJECTS:
Private Residences: Los Angeles, Beverly Hills, Brentwood, Bel Air, Palm Desert and San Francisco, California; New York, New York; North Carolina; China; and Indonesia.

Commercial Work:
Furniture showroom in North Carolina; contract interiors in Los Angeles, Las Vegas, New York, London, Malaysia and Indonesia.

CREDENTIALS:
Harvard University, Master of Architecture
University of Southern California, B.S., Architecture
Registered Architect, California
American Institute of Architects, Member

PUBLISHED IN:
Architectural Digest
Architectural Record
Angeles Magazine

BELOW: Custom furniture designs for sofa, chairs, coffee tables, end tables, wood screen and projection chandelier. Custom fabric treatments on columns, custom light trough, custom modular wall finish. (custom furniture fabrications by Barry Salehian)

*LEFT: Serene colors characterize
a quiet sitting area.*

*BELOW: Custom copper wall
panels cast intriguing reflections
from behind a custom buffet
cabinet.*

MICHAEL C.F. CHAN & ASSOCIATES, INC.

RIGHT: Antique furnishings off-set the rigid concrete and steel of the skyline.

BELOW LEFT: Elliptical space with a custom vanity table complements a discovered antique bench. (custom furniture by Barry Salehian)

BELOW RIGHT: Custom executive desk blends with traditional heavy wood panel work. (custom furniture fabrication by Barry Salehian)

PHILOSOPHY:
Our approach to interior design is defined through an architectural background with a strong emphasis on form, space, light quality and materials. Often we create custom designs for furniture, wall treatments, light fixtures, linens and accessories which define the character of the space, creating a sense of "place." Each project is viewed as one design; each part is complementary to the whole, integrating both interior design and architecture into "interior architecture."

ABOVE LEFT: A fireplace defines the space, while custom shelving gives variety and texture to the walls.

BELOW LEFT: Clean and simple details, materials and lighting create a contemporary environment.

COLAVITO LEVINE
INTERIOR DESIGN
FIRM

PHILIP COLAVITO
Los Angeles: 213-662-8850
PALM SPRINGS: 619-416-2358

ANDREW LEVINE

BELOW: Comfort in this contemporary living room is achieved through a mixture of Regency, French and neoclassical styles in California scale. The space lends itself to the traditional functions of a living room, as well as informal fireside dining.

ABOVE: Designed specifically
for the "Eye On Design"
exhibition at the Pacific Design
Center, this space incorporates
aluminum walls with a tortoise
shell finish, a customized poster
bed designed by C/L, two
Eighteenth Century terrazzo and
steel side tables, art deco peer
paintings, an Egyptian slipper
stool, as well as French and
Neo-Classical furnishings.
Fabrics are of raw silk, chemise
and linen.

COLAVITO LEVINE
INTERIOR DESIGN
FIRM

PROJECTS:
Private Residences: Los Angeles, Malibu and Palm Springs, California; Boston; Darian, Connecticut and Manhattan.

Commercial Work: Maguire Thomas Partners, Hyatt Hotels, Mitsui Fusodan, M.S. Management, M.G.M. and Fox.

CREDENTIALS:
ISID, associate member
Los Angeles Society of Interior Designers
Sagewood Development, Divine Design
    Architectural Committee, sponsor
    and featured design firm
UCLA School of Architecture and Design
Divine Design sponsor and featured
    design firm

PUBLISHED IN:
The Wall Street Journal
Los Angeles Business Journal
Television Appearances
CBS Evening News
Los Angeles Fox affiliate

PHILOSOPHY:
The client's comfort level during the design process is as important as the selection of furnishings and materials. We have never dictated design to our clients. We simply help translate their own style and taste into the appropriate balance between function and beauty. When a project is completed, we give our clients a gift – the gift of pleasure emanating from every corner of their surroundings.

LEFT: This richly ornate headboard uses antique fabric and gold-threaded saris for unexpected drama.

OPPOSITE: The strong character of the living room in this Palm Springs home once owned by Clark Gable lends itself to intimate candle light, luxurious fabric, antique rugs and exotic furnishings from around the world. Throughout the entire compound we tried to create the mood one would experience in a villa on the hillsides of Tuscany.

GLENNA COOK
INTERIORS

GLENNA COOK
132 E. THIRD AVE.
SAN MATEO, CA 94401
(415)342-5089   FAX (415)342-3995

PROJECTS:
Private Residences and Commercial
Work: San Francisco and Los Angeles;
Vail, Colorado; Chicago; Miami; Japan;
Hong Kong; Norway; and South
America.

CREDENTIALS:
Simmons College, Boston
UC Berkeley Extension

PUBLISHED IN:
Sunset Books
San Francisco Chronicle
San Francisco Examiner
San Jose Mercury
Home Magazine
HG "Remodeling Issue"

PHILOSOPHY:
I consider myself a designer rather than
a decorator. There must be a practical
sense to the planning and flow of any
room. Whether newly built or remodeled,
houses must be functional and
convenient.

   Decorating and furnishings are simply
finishing touches that appeal to the
clients' tastes. This part of the job can't
be neglected, however, because the
decorating is what everyone sees.

   I take great pride concerning the total
look, much as an artist considers his
canvas.

*ABOVE LEFT: Abundant work
area helps give this kitchen a
degree of functionality that
matches its inviting design.*

*LEFT: A striking poster bed
exaggerates the height of a room
that already seems to soar.*

LEFT: A sense of uncluttered spaciousness paves the way for the practical flow of this contemporary apartment.

BELOW: Unpretentious furnishings contrast with distinctive accessories to set the stage for a magnificent view of the San Francisco skyline.

COLIN COWIE
LIFESTYLE, INC.

COLIN COWIE
316 N. ROSSMORE AVENUE, SUITE 601
LOS ANGELES, CA 90004
(213)462-7183

PROJECTS:
Private Residences: Los Angeles; New York; Pennsylvania; London; South Africa; Hong Kong; and Saudi Arabia.

Commercial work: Restaurants, nightclubs, movie theaters, and hotels in Los Angeles; Sun Valley, Idaho; Melbourne, Australia; South Africa and Costa Rica.

PUBLISHED IN:
House & Garden
Los Angeles Times
In Style
People
USA Today

APPEARANCES:
Entertainment Tonight
HG TV
Rooms for Improvement
Awesome Interior
CNN
Home Show
Good Morning America

PHILOSOPHY:
Function is as important as design. All aspects of a living space should be geared toward comfort, with the design enhancing the client's lifestyle. Details make the difference.

LEFT: The color ox blood was mixed with bordeaux to create a more intimate surrounding in an existing small space. Strong yet practical pieces make this study one of his client's favorite rooms.

OPPOSITE LEFT: Casual elegance compliments this California Mediterranean Pied-a-Tierre. Colors were kept in the cool tones such as latte instead of vibrant white. The light tones and dark accessories balance the room against the height of the 20' ceiling.

OPPOSITE RIGHT: Detailed mahogany cabinetry frames the pistachio walls into a functional yet beautiful city kitchen for one of Los Angeles's famous chefs.

BELOW OPPOSITE: Soft colors and fabrics create a room that's easy to curl up in. Using antiques and new pieces of furniture creates a subtle balance between harmony and elegance.

DAVID DALTON ASSOCIATES

DAVID DALTON, ASID
OFFICE/SHOWROOM:
PACIFIC DESIGN CENTER
8687 MELROSE AVENUE #G290
LOS ANGELES, CA 90069
(213)340-8342

RIGHT: An over-mantel porthole mirror reflects the image of custom furnishings.

BELOW: An oversized paper lantern lights the beech table and chairs in a casually elegant dining room.

OPPOSITE: A handsome ajero wood folding screen creates an architectural backdrop for custom furnishings in the living room of this Beverly Hills home.

DAVID DALTON ASSOCIATES

ABOVE LEFT: Custom iron drapery finials complement unique window treatments.

ABOVE RIGHT: A coffee table stained with rich Moroccan henna holds two rare Spanish colonial santos.

RIGHT: A collection of antique Chinese storage vessels and a bronze bust rest on an oversized, hand-carved wood and granite console.

OPPOSITE: Specially designed iron window screens and hand-stenciled floors transform this California living room into a cozy retreat.

PROJECTS:
Private Residences: Los Angeles, Beverly Hills, San Marino, Santa Barbara, Laguna and La Jolla, California; Chicago; and New York.

Commercial Work: Executive offices, restaurants, retail stores, manufacturers' showrooms, hotels and a line of custom furnishings.

CREDENTIALS:
ASID, Professional Member
Certified Interior Designer
Design Group Los Angeles
Divine Design 1994, 1995
Designers Lighting Forum

PHILOSOPHY:
Meis Van Dereoh said it best: "God is in the details."

DESIGN VISIONS

KATHLEEN P. DOONAN
13900 TAHITI WAY #124
MARINA DEL REY, CA 90292
(310)821-7712 FAX (310)821-1703

PROJECTS:
Private Residences: Newport Beach, Laguna, Beverly Hills, Palm Springs and San Francisco, California; New York City; Colorado; New Jersey; Connecticut; Arkansas; Nevada and Florida.

Commercial Work: Law and business offices in California and New York; restaurants in California and hotels in Florida and California.

CREDENTIALS:
ASID, IFDA
Moore College of Art, Philadelphia
Parsons School of Design, New York

ABOVE OPPOSITE: Bright patterns contrast with the deep finish of the carved furnishings to create a bedroom that seems to have been lifted from a Southern mansion.

BELOW OPPOSITE: Ingenious wall coverings and Romanesque design elements turn this master bedroom into a land of fantasy and intrigue.

LEFT: Elaborate patterns in the upholstery, rug and wall hanging give a museum-quality appearance to this striking dining room.

BELOW: Comfortable furniture groupings transform a large open area into a series of intimate spaces that retain a sense of generous scale.

RODGER F. DOBBEL
23 VISTA AVE.
PIEDMONT, CA 94611
(510)654-6723   FAX (510)658-7556

RODGER DOBBEL
INTERIORS

PHILOSOPHY:
Through the creative use of light, color, texture and scale, I seek to reflect the client's lifestyle in a sensitive manner.
Quality workmanship and attention to detail add warmth and livability to any design project, while good business ethics ensure that it will be a rewarding experience for both client and designer.

PROJECTS:
Private Residences: San Francisco, Palm Springs, Newport Beach, Los Angeles and Santa Monica, California; New York; and New Jersey.

CREDENTIALS:
ASID, Professional Member
Chouinard Art Institute
Baron's Who's Who in Interior Design
Baron's Who's Who in Interior Design, International Edition
Marqui's Who's Who in the West
Marqui's Who's Who in the World
National Philanthropy Day Distinquished Volunteer Honoree Award, 1990

PUBLISHED IN:
House Beautiful
HG
HG, Kitchen & Bath
Better Homes & Gardens Decorating Ideas
Gourmet
Interior Design
Designers West
Showcase of Interior Design
100 Designers' Favorite Rooms

*ABOVE LEFT:
A sleek, polished steel-and-granite console, an antique Chinese philosopher, and lacquered Chippendale rococo chairs enhance the beauty of a dramatic coromandel screen.*

BELOW LEFT: A contemporary painting creates a wonderful backdrop for a mix of French and Chinese antiques.

OPPOSITE: Rich textures of neutral and black introduce subtle style to a casual sitting room in northern California. Traditional upholstery and gloss lacquer pieces accent the antique Japanese two-panel screen.

GUS DUFFY A.I.A.
ARCHITECT

GUS DUFFY
11333 MOORPARK ST., #455
TOLUCA LAKE, CA 91602
(818)509-0505 FAX (818)509-7847

CREDENTIALS:
AIA
Licensed architect in California, Colorado, Hawaii
University of Notre Dame, bachelor of architecture

PUBLICATIONS:
Architectural Digest
Designers West
Forbes
Los Angeles Times

PROJECTS:
Private Residences: Los Angeles, Beverly Hills and Malibu, California; Telluride, Aspen, Steamboat Springs and Mancos, Colorado; and Kauai, Hawaii.

Commercial Work: Junior League Headquarters, Los Angeles; Sepulveda House historic restoration, Los Angeles; and Mission Street Plaza, San Marino, California.

PHILOSOPHY:
I listen closely to what clients say, and remain involved in all facets of a project, from concept discussions and sketch sessions to final interior details.

I aim for lively, vigorous design solutions full of historical and regional allusions. My clients provide the clues – usually a few key details, but sometimes elaborate ideas – which we then develop into reality.

RIGHT: Sunlight from the east floods an exquisite master bath that's perhaps better described as a "private morning room."

BELOW OPPOSITE: Plenty of furnishings and relatively little cabinetry allows this kitchen to meet the client's desire for a wide-open family gathering place.

BELOW: Pine plank floors, colorful throw rugs and a rich beamed ceiling set the background for the blues and whites in the countertops, backsplashes and cabinets.

DONNA DUNN &
ASSOCIATES

DONNA DUNN, ASID
73-230 FIDDLENECK LANE
PALM DESERT, CA 92260
(619)340-9598 FAX (619)568-1968

PROJECTS:
Private Residences: Maryland;
Virginia; Washington, D.C.; Vancouver,
Washington; Beverly Hills, Brentwood,
Los Angeles, Palm Desert, Indian Wells
and Rancho Mirage, California.

Commercial Work: Washington, D.C.,
offices of CBS; model homes, professional offices and health care facilities in
metropolitan Washington, D.C.

*TOP: Rich taupe walls and wool
and sisal carpeting envelope this
master bedroom with warmth.
The pine four poster bed is
anchored by an old kilim rug
and antique trunk.*

*ABOVE: A cast-stone
fireplace and ceiling beams
add architectural interest to an
eclectic living room. The informal conversation area features
subtle earth tones combined
with a variety of textures in the
fabrics, area rug and window
coverings.*

*OPPOSITE: Precise lighting and
an overscaled abstract painting
by New York artist Robert
Natkin create a dramatic setting
for informal dining.*

DONNA DUNN & ASSOCIATES

CREDENTIALS:
ASID, Professional Member
President: 1995-1996, Palm Springs
  Chapter, ASID
Certified in California, #0935
Director of Interior Design,
  Bloomingdale's, Tysons Corner, Virginia

PHILOSOPHY:
I try to bring to every project a feeling that is both inviting and comfortable, not only physically, but psychologically as well. Whether the client is looking for a casual elegance or something more formal, the home is a place to "feel good." I try to help clients interpret their likes and dislikes so that the end result is something I can feel proud of and is a true reflection of their taste and lifestyle. The interior design and decoration of a home should be a fun, enjoyable experience, and I feel it's my job to make it that way.

LEFT: A custom glass wall separates the main entry of this desert estate from the family room. The furnishings also were custom designed to accommodate casual living. (Project co-designed by Kristine Schultz, ASID.)

BELOW: Color and texture bring warmth to a small gentleman's library that is as relaxed as the cougar painting by artist Richard Murray.

OPPOSITE: The stepping of the perimeter walls in the main entry of the 1995 Desert Showcase House prompts natural curiosity for what lies beyond, while providing the perfect foil for custom-designed furnishings and contemporary art.

EDWARD C. TURRENTINE INTERIOR DESIGN INC.

EDWARD C. TURRENTINE
70 N. RAYMOND AVE.
PASADENA, CA 91103
(818)795-9964   FAX (818)795-0027

PROJECTS:
Private Residences: Throughout the country, from California to Maine.

CREDENTIALS:
ASID, professional member
Woodbury University

LEFT: The ballroom in this Pasadena residence features a sweeping iron staircase, 18th century reproduction pilasters, and flowing draperies that aspire to the 28-foot ceiling.

BELOW: Iron work on the French-style doors exemplifies the detail found throughout this Italianate mansion.

BOTTOM: Cream stone details and a limestone floor accentuate soft upholstered furnishings.

OPPOSITE: Original plaster ornamentation on the ceiling and frieze embellishes a timeless dining room with flowers by Jerry Palmer.

EDWARD C. TURRENTINE INTERIOR DESIGN INC.

PHILOSOPHY:
My designs emphasize architectural details. I borrow from the past and stretch toward the future to give form to the imagination of my clients and create rooms that are uniquely their own. Custom furniture and fine moldings are among the details I bring into play to reflect a client's taste and produce timeless designs.

FAR LEFT: Strong architectural elements form the roots of an inviting garden.

LEFT: Subtle color and rich wood tones set the theme in a magnificently appointed master bedroom.

BELOW: French furnishings and architectural details add grandeur to a spacious sitting area. Note the custom cord and tassels on the French empire sofa.

OPPOSITE: Glass block skylights illuminate a conservatory with an arched ribbed ceiling. The mural adds depth and interest.

ELISABETH LUCE
INTERIORS

ELISABETH LUCE
3476 JACKSON ST.
SAN FRANCISCO, CA 94118
PHONE/FAX (415)922-7851

PROJECTS:
Private Residences: Governor's
residence, Albany, New York; Long
Island, New York; Far Hills, New Jersey;
Greenwich, Connecticut; Shaker Heights,
Ohio; Kennebunkport, Maine; Delray
Beach, Florida; Portland, Oregon; and
Marin County and San Francisco,
California.

CREDENTIALS:
New York School of Interior Design
San Francisco Decorator Showcase,
  1989, 1990
San Francisco DIFFA Showcase, 1989

PUBLISHED IN:
Better Homes & Gardens
Interiors & Sources
Northern California Home & Garden
House Beautiful

PHILOSOPHY:
I'm a traditionalist, but one who likes
to mix a dash of the new and original
into my designs. My inspiration comes
from color, pattern, and the personalities
and lifestyles of my clients.
  I love to layer colors, patterns, rich
fabrics, heavy draperies and antiques to
create warm, welcoming interiors where
comfort is uppermost. My favorite
periods include neoclassical and rococo,
with a strong preference for English and
Continental furniture.

*ABOVE: Tradition abounds in
a charming vignette that seems
borrowed from yesterday.*

*ABOVE OPPOSITE: Carefully
chosen accessories add the
finishing touches to a visually
enticing room.*

*OPPOSITE: The eclectic interplay
between color and texture
creates a cheerful living area
that avoids being overly formal.
Note how the contemporary
artwork over the sofa contrasts
with – yet complements – the
traditional furnishings.*

ENOS & CO. -
MAYHEW DESIGN

MARK ENOS
ENOS & COMPANY
705 NORTH ALFRED STREET
LOS ANGELES, CA 90069
(213)655-0109 FAX (213)655-7719

RICHARD MAYHEW
MAYHEW DESIGN
705 NORTH ALFRED STREET
LOS ANGELES, CA 90069
(213)655-0109 FAX (213)655-7719

PHILOSOPHY:
Our shared design focus is to create a comfortable, yet stylized, living environment unique to each client's taste and needs. Beginning with an architectural concept that is both beautiful and simplistic, we are free to design in a variety of styles.

ABOVE: An eclectic mixture of traditional and contemporary furnishings and artwork creates a warm, cozy room – a reflection of the designers' personal taste.

OPPOSITE: Built for the King of Spain, this 1920s home features rich Moroccan architecture that influenced the design of the master suite. A grand bed with antique stone columns is the centerpiece of the room. Golden Venetian plaster walls and dramatic lighting add to the ambiance.

ENOS & CO. - MAYHEW DESIGN

OPPOSITE: A Palladian villa recreated on the 25th floor of a modern office tower welcomes travelers to an intimate European experience in the Hotel Hankyu International in Osaka, Japan.

ABOVE LEFT: This 1920s bath in the Venice Family Clinic Design House in Bel-Air, California was renovated and modernized with an elliptical mahogany vanity, tubular lighting and a marble mosaic floor. The golden wall tile was restored to the full beauty of its original color.

ABOVE RIGHT: A book-lined alcove provides an intimate area for reading or quiet conversation in the library of the Hotel Hankyu International in Osaka, Japan.

BELOW: A warm family retreat in a Beverly Hills, California residence that mixes traditional and contemporary furnishings and materials. Note the dramatic painting by Pat Stear.

SANNENE
GAREHIME
INTERIORS

SANNENE GAREHIME
15 BIRD'S NEST COURT
MILL VALLEY, CA 94941
(415)389-5451 FAX (415)389-1946

PROJECTS:
Private Residences: Palm Springs,
Atherton, Marin County, Sonoma County
and Sacramento, California; and Las
Vegas.

PHILOSOPHY:
Homes should inspire and rejuvenate,
while mirroring the hearts and souls of
their owners. Each of my designs are
individually unique as are my clients.

*RIGHT: Dramatic window
dressings emphasize the scale
of this formal dining room. The
interplay of color and texture
provides warmth, while an
innovative table dressing adds
further elegance.*

*OPPOSITE: A turn-of-the-
century Victorian home meets
the needs of a family with a
contemporary lifestyle. Note
how the room's architectural
influences are enhanced by the
textural fern paper inset into the
wall moldings and the unique
application of silver leaf on the
heavy crown molding.*

GERHARD
DESIGN GROUP

ANDREW H. GERHARD, ASID
7630 EL CAMINO REAL
RANCHO LA COSTA, CA 92009
(619)436-0181   FAX (619)436-7945

PROJECTS:
Private Residences: Beverly Hills, Malibu, Palm Springs, La Jolla, La Costa, Rancho Santa Fe and Del Mar, California; Sun Valley, Idaho; Denver; Chicago; St. Louis; New York; Mexico; Brazil; and Canada.

Commercial Work: Prime Sports Network, Los Angeles; Cablevision, Carlsbad, California; Daniels Communications, Inc., Denver; Pisces Restaurant and La Costa Hotel & Spa, Rancho La Costa, California; and corporate offices, restaurants, resorts and country clubs throughout the United States and abroad.

CREDENTIALS:
ASID, Professional Member
Barron's Who's Who in Interior Design, 1988-95
Advisory Board Member, University of California, San Diego, Interior Design Program

BELOW: A breathtaking chandelier, brilliant artwork and some of the world's finest materials frame a visual feast in an unforgettable entry.

OPPOSITE: Contemporary furnishings and accessories introduce a casually sophisticated feel to a space that features striking architectural elements.

GERHARD
DESIGN GROUP

RIGHT: A wall of mirrors dramatically opens up a narrow, functional space that combines sleep, work and entertainment.

BELOW: Rich colors, exquisite furnishings and an abundance of architectural details work together to create the ultimate in refined living. Note the trompe l'oeil "alcoves" on the right.

PUBLISHED IN:
Architectural Digest
Audio-Video Interiors
Designers West
Business Interiors
HG
San Diego Magazine
Interiors
House Beautiful
Town & Country
San Diego Home/Garden

PHILOSOPHY:
Through the creative use of design, interiors should communicate a mood or philosophy. Architecture and design must be integrated to achieve balance in any space. Only by working as a team can designer and client obtain the ultimate design success.

LEFT: Generously scaled artwork and intriguing angles are among the discoveries available around every corner.

BELOW: Stunning interior design rivals the beauty of the natural environment in a space that offers the promise of pampering inside and out.

GARY S. GIBSON

GARY GIBSON
146 NORTH SWALL DRIVE
LOS ANGELES, CA 90048
(310)274-9622   FAX (310)274-1417

PROJECTS:
Private Residences: Brentwood, Beverly
Hills and San Marino, California; Santa
Fe, New Mexico; Las Vegas, Nevada;
and Park City, Utah.

Commercial Work:
Westwood and Hollywood, California.

*BELOW: Fine artwork
provides a striking counterpoint
to the wooden ceiling beams,
stone fireplace and comfortable
furnishings in this rustic living
area.*

*OPPOSITE: Broad arches
and high ceilings evoke the
expansive mood of a castle, a
mood that's both complemented
and contrasted by eclectic
furnishings and artwork.*

LEFT: A mixture of textures, materials, colors and periods gives this sitting area a number of personalities - all of them comfortable.

BELOW: Natural materials bring subdued color to a sophisticated living area.

RIGHT: Dramatically simple style creates an uncluttered look that still provides several interesting focal points.

BELOW: Uncommonly warm and cheerful, this inviting room seems to float between indoors and out.

HARTE-BROWNLEE
& ASSOCIATES INC.

SHELDON M. HARTE, ASID
1691 WESTCLIFF DRIVE
NEWPORT BEACH, CA 92660
(714)548-9530 FAX (714)548-9528

JOHN M. BROWNLEE

PROJECTS:
Private Residences: U.S. Embassy residence, Singapore; Newport Beach, Laguna Beach, Beverly Hills, Vintage Indian Wells, San Marino, Pasadena, Pacific Palisades, San Francisco and Lake Tahoe, California; Deer Valley, Utah; and Hawaii.

Commercial Work: Pacific Investment Management Co. and PIMCO Advisors L.P., Newport Beach, California; Pacific Mutual, chairman's office; Smith International; Nabors Cadillac, Buick and Spreen Honda automobile dealerships.

CREDENTIALS:
ASID, Allied Member
Pasadena Showcase House of Design, 1989-1996
ASID Orange County Philharmonic House of Design, 1996

PUBLISHED IN:
HG
Designers West
L.A. Style
Southern California Home & Garden
California Homes & Lifestyles
Orange County
L.A. Times

PHILOSOPHY:
Helping our clients interpret their wants, needs and desires is the first step toward turning a house into a home. Regardless of their specific style, residential environments should be both attractive and comfortable.

BELOW: An antique Chinese rug sets the palette for this sophisticated living room influenced by the Orient.

OPPOSITE: This inviting library is warmed by rich cherry paneling, soft chenilles and silks and complemented by an impressionist masterpiece above the fireplace.

HARTE-BROWNLEE & ASSOCIATES INC.

RIGHT: A primitive collection of antiques accents the family room in this Mediterranean oceanfront home. An 18th century gypsy cart serves as the coffee table and complements the rustic ceiling beams.

BELOW: An extension of the living quarters hovers over the Pacific, providing the perfect spot to enjoy a relaxing sunset.

ABOVE OPPOSITE: A beautiful draped bed turns this master bedroom into a room within a room.

BELOW OPPOSITE: An 18th century carved limestone fireplace warms the living room of this contemporary Laguna Beach home. Generous furnishings and sumptuous fabrics create an ideal area for entertaining.

MURIEL HEBERT,
INC.

MURIEL HEBERT
TONI THURLING
117 SHERIDAN AVE.
PIEDMONT, CA 94611
(510)547-1294

PROJECTS:
San Francisco Bay area, Carmel and
Sacramento, California; and Lake Tahoe,
Nevada.

Commercial Work: Executive offices,
conference rooms, reception areas and
private clubs.

CREDENTIALS:
Rudolph Schaeffer School of Design
San Francisco Decorator Showcase
Piedmont Designer Showcase
Hillsborough Designer Showcase

PUBLISHED IN:
Architectural Digest
HG
House Beautiful
Town & Country
Designers West
Interior Design
San Francisco Examiner
Oakland Tribune

RON HEFLER

RONALD F. HEFLER
465 S. SWEETZER AVENUE
LOS ANGELES, CA 90048
(213)651-1231   FAX (213)735-2502

PROJECTS:
Private Residences: Los Angeles, Beverly Hills, Bel-Air, Brentwood, Malibu, San Francisco and Palm Springs, California; Tucson, Arizona; ski resort residence, Deer Valley, Utah; New York, New York; and Mexico City and Puerto Vallarta, Mexico.

Commercial Work: Executive offices in Los Angeles and Beverly Hills, California; The Beverly Hills Hotel; Walt Disney Studios; Paramount Pictures; and Twentieth Century Fox.

CREDENTIALS:
University of Illinois, B.A.
Art Institute, Chicago

PUBLISHED IN:
HG
Interior Visions
House Beautiful
Los Angeles Times
Designers West
Interiors

PHILOSOPHY:
The combined roles of the designer and client today have evolved into a very personal and professional enterprise. My responsibility is to combine the best of my clients' increasingly sophisticated taste with the dictates of the job, thereby creating an environment that is beautiful, functional, architecturally detailed and full of the creative expression that each client and commission deserves.

ABOVE LEFT: Subtle Southwestern motifs and warm colorations set the stage in this den/library.

LEFT: An intimate fireplace area combines wood and stone with warm, jewel-toned colorations in the antique area rug and occasional seating.

OPPOSITE: A mix of ethnic furnishings and accessories, including a rare set of carved wood English animal heads, highlights the massive living room wall in this Deer Valley, Utah, residence.

RON HEFLER

LEFT: The mix of taupes, tans and creams with black accents results in a sophisticated setting.

BELOW: A mirrored fireplace wall encompasses an architectural mirror and reflects beauty all around.

OPPOSITE: Green and white slipcovers help create an expression of summer in this seasonal living room.

ALBERT JANZ AND SHERRY STEIN
95 SAN MIGUEL ROAD
PASADENA, CA 91105
(818)716-7624

CREDENTIALS:
Henry Johnstone & Co.:
Pasadena Showcase House of Design,
  1993-1995
ISID/Joffrey Ballet Design House, 1992
Sandpiper Design house, 1989
ISID International Design House, 1982

Albert Janz:
School of Visual Arts, New York
UCLA
International Interior Design Association

Sherry Stein:
Occidental College, B.A.
Art Institute of Southern California

HENRY JOHNSTONE & CO.

TOP: Tiles from the 1920s inspired the decoration of this guest bath.

LEFT: A demilune console and stately mirror enhance a hall alcove. The antique prints are applied directly to the walls.

OPPOSITE: A custom-designed, Gothic-style mirror hangs above an early 18th century chest of drawers. Complementing the architecture is a wainscot inscribed with a trefoil pattern.

HENRY JOHNSTONE & CO.

RIGHT: A corona surmounts the bed to become the focal point in a room that includes custom-printed chintz and antique furnishings.

BELOW: A Gothic revival sitting room is born by vaulting a previously flat ceiling and adding cabinetry and moldings.

OPPOSITE: Old World tile enlivens a small flower sink.

IN-SITE DESIGN
GROUP INC.

COLLEEN JOHNSON

JUDY GUBNER

CREDENTIALS:
ASID, Professional Member
ASID Board of Directors, Colorado chapter
Colorado Institute of Art, A.A.
NCIDQ certified
Parade of Homes, judge
The Taste of Cherry Creek,
  event designer

3551 S. MONACO PKWY., SUITE 208
DENVER, CO 80237
(303)691-9000   FAX (303)757-6475

CREDENTIALS:
ASID, Professional Member
ASID Board of Directors, Colorado chapter
Wheaton College (Massachusetts), B.A.
University of Colorado, School of
  Architecture & Planning, M.A.
NCIDQ certified
The Denver Design Center,
  advisory board
Parade of Homes, judge
The Taste of Cherry Creek,
  event designer

IN-SITE DESIGN GROUP INC.

PROJECTS:
Private Residences: Throughout the
United States.

Commercial Work: Hotel public spaces
and guest suites, professional offices,
retail facilities, government training
centers and model homes.

PUBLISHED IN:
Interiors & Sources
Luxury Homes
Timber Frame Homes
Colorado Homes & Lifestyles
Country Homes

PHILOSOPHY:
We present photographs of interiors
that speak for themselves, that capture
and portray our philosophy of design.
These real rooms, functional and lived-
in, are the result of a special alchemy:
selecting and combining, arranging and
balancing the myriad elements that form
unique spaces for living, growing,
relaxing, collecting, entertaining.

From the intricate detailing of a custom
designed and crafted hand rail to the
restoration of a family heirloom; from
the faithful reproduction of New Mexican
Territorial Style to the collaborative
realization of an architect's vision, we
take pride in creating interiors that mirror
their owners and reflect their regions.
Our definition of success is when a
client's friends exclaim, "This looks just
like you!"

As co-creators with our clients much
of the joy of our work comes from never
knowing what we might do next...

KERRY JOYCE
ASSOCIATES INC.

KERRY JOYCE
115 NORTH LA BREA AVENUE
LOS ANGELES, CA 90036
(213)938-4442

PROJECTS:
Private Residences: Interior architecture
and interior design for residences in New
York and Beverly Hills, Newport Beach,
Palm Springs and Pasadena, California.

Product Design: Designer of Architectural
Fireplace Mantels and Kerry Joyce
Furniture Collection for James Jennings
Furniture.

CREDENTIALS:
CCIDC Certified Interior Designer
Emmy Award for Set Decoration
New York University, B.F.A.
Society of Motion Picture & Television
  Art Directors
Featured in *Metropolitan Home's*
  "*Design 100*" issue, 1992
Residential design award, *Interiors*
  magazine, 1994
Chosen as one of 16 designers for the
  Getty House, official residence of the
  mayor of Los Angeles

PUBLISHED IN:
Elle Decor
House Beautiful
House & Garden
Interior Design
Los Angeles Times
Metropolitan Home
New York Times
Town & Country
World of Interiors

KERRY JOYCE
ASSOCIATES INC.

PHILOSOPHY:
Kerry Joyce's interiors are characterized by a love for detail and fine materials. Able to work in a broad range of styles, he deftly creates satisfying interiors that reflect the personalities and lifestyles of his clients. "I love good design as well as comfort and I take it as a challenge to create an interior that will satisfy both." He believes strongly in the integration of architecture and interior design - having an affinity for both. "I reject trend or fad. Creating a timeless, enduring interior is very important to me."

JULIE LANTERMAN
INTERIOR DESIGNS

JULIE LANTERMAN
5 ST. FRANCIS ROAD
HILLSBOROUGH, CA 94010
(415)348-3823   FAX (415)348-3823

PROJECTS:
Private Residences: Hillsborough,
Atherton, San Francisco, Carmel and
West Hollywood, California; and Maui,
Hawaii.

Commercial Work: Rehabilitation home
in San Francisco, California, and medical
center in Palo Alto, California.

PUBLISHED IN:
Various San Francisco Bay area
publications

CREDENTIALS:
ASID, Allied Member
Hillsborough Decorators Showhouse,
 Since 1983
Historic "Carolands" Showcase, 1991
Celebrations of Christmas, San Francisco
 Design Center, 1991
Dickens House, 1990-95
CSL Kitchen Tour, 1992-95

*LEFT: A newly created alcove
frames a Chippendale-style
mirror and a lion's head
pedestal sink in this restructured
powder room.*

*BELOW: Hand-painted glazed
walls, silk lined damask draped
windows and a 19th century
French chandelier set the stage
for entertaining meals.*

*OPPOSITE: Lavish dinner parties
originate from this spectacular
backdrop.*

JULIE LANTERMAN INTERIOR DESIGNS

PHILOSOPHY:

Successful design provides artistic, functional, pleasurable and well-planned living areas that meet the unique requirements of each client. People should be surrounded by beautiful things. The challenge is to harmonize beauty and realistic living environments.

Quality craftsmanship, knowledge of construction, attention to architectural detail, and sharp listening skills are among the resources I share with clients to help fulfill their vision.

RIGHT: The hand carved, white oak archway serves as a transition between working and eating areas, while accommodating the stainless steel double ovens.

BELOW: A combination library and formal family room offers a palette inspired by the 1930s Morharjeran Sarouk rug. The custom cherry woodwork creates a warm and inviting living area.

OPPOSITE: Inspired by the French countryside, this garden kitchen features marble, natural woods and hand-painted walls.

KATHLEEN FORMANACK & ASSOCIATES INTERIOR DESIGN & CONSTRUCTION DEVELOPMENT

LEFT: Silk walls, intricate gilded moldings and a mirrored ceiling bring new life to a formerly drab dressing room. The drapery rod is from a Chinese altar piece. Pasadena Showcase House of Design.

BELOW: Eight custom tile patterns lend a unique quality to the tub, walls and sink in this teenager's bathroom. The walls are covered in black suede, and the base and crown moldings are accented in gold and nickel leaf.

KATHLEEN FORMANACK ASID, CID
608 W. LEMON AVE.
ARCADIA, CA 91007
(818)447-9157   FAX (818)447-3546

PROJECTS:
Private Residences: California.

Commercial Work: California.

CREDENTIALS:
Circle of Excellence Award, AA Design
 & Merchandising
ASID Regional Board Member
Certified interior designer
Baron's Who's Who in Interior Design
International Directory of
 Distinguished Leadership
Pasadena Showcase House of Design

PUBLISHED IN:
Audio Video Interiors
Home & Garden
Los Angeles Times

PHILOSOPHY:
Encouraging clients to stretch their vision is a great adventure. Often clients want change, but they don't know how to arrive at it.
   The beginning of each project involves interpreting the desires and dreams of the client. Learning what they don't like is as important as discovering what they do like. If the groundwork is laid properly early on, the end of each project will be filled with "oohs and aahs."

LEFT: Pale shades of apricot, champagne and blue set the mood in a palatial estate at Ritz Cove, Monarch Beach.

BELOW: A 70's basement disco was remodeled into an entertainment area. The projection TV and dance floor lights add visual interest. Pasadena Showcase House of Design.

ELLEN
LEMER
KORNEY
ASSOCIATES

ELLEN LEMER KORNEY, ASID
10170 CULVER BOULEVARD
CULVER CITY, CA 90232
(310)204-6576   FAX (310)204-1457

PROJECTS:
Private Residences: Beverly Hills, Bel-Air, Los Angeles, Sherman Oaks and San Francisco, California; New York City, Westchester, East Hampton, Quoque and West Hampton, New York; and Boca Raton and Miami, Florida.

Commercial Work: New York City cooperatives (public spaces); accounting, law and executive offices in New York and Los Angeles.

CREDENTIALS:
ASID, Professional Member
California Certified Interior Designer
New York School of Design
Parsons School of Design
Baron's Who's Who in Interior Design
First Place, Residential ASID/LA Design
  Competition

PUBLISHED IN:
Designing For Comfort
Interior Designers Showcase of Color
Very Small Living Spaces
The Designer
Home Entertainment
House Beautiful
L.A. West
Manhattan Living

PHILOSOPHY:
Timeless design, quality and attention to detail are essential to creating beautiful living and working environments. An effective designer listens and interprets clients' needs and dreams. From blueprints to project completion, designing is a dialogue and an educational process.

ABOVE TOP: Black absolute granite flooring, a mirrored wall and a faux antique limestone wall transform a narrow, low-ceiling cinder block entry.

ABOVE: French Boiserie paneling, a custom Hunt desk, and elegant cotton damask and bargello fabrics add warmth and comfort to a gentleman's library.

OPPOSITE: A skylight and Palladian window spread light on the antique rug and country pieces in this cozy master bedroom loft.

PAT LARIN
INTERIORS

PAT LARIN, ASID
12720 DIANNE DRIVE
LOS ALTOS, CA 94022
(415)941-4611 FAX (415)941-4047

CREDENTIALS:
ASID, Professional Member
Cornell University, B.S.
Licensed General Contractor
Certified Interior Designer
San Francisco Bay Area
   Showhouses (12)
Numerous ASID Design Awards
Who's Who in Interior Design

PUBLISHED IN:
Gentry Magazine
Gentry Design
Designers Illustrated
Better Homes & Gardens
HG
Home
Windows & Walls
Kitchens & Baths'
West Magazine
San Francisco Chronicle
San Jose Mercury News
South Bay Accent
San Francisco Focus
100 Designers' Favorite Rooms

PHILOSOPHY:
We provide design and remodeling
services to a wide range of residential
and corporate clients. Our attention to
detail and commitment to delivering
unique projects and outstanding service
have put us at the top of our field. From
concept to completion, all aspects of
the design process are professionally
planned, scheduled and supervised
because we are a highly trained team
with vast resources at our fingertips.

Our blueprint for design excellence
resonates with appropriateness, balance,
harmony and proportion. Each
environment blends our creativity with
our dedication to the special needs,
tastes and preferences of our clients.
Whether contemporary or traditional –
or a tasteful blend of both – our spaces
are always appropriate, classic, timeless,
comfortable and nurturing, with an
understated, relaxed elegance.

LECZINSKI DESIGN
ASSOCIATES

DENNIS LECZINSKI, FASID
115 MADISON STREET
DENVER, CO 80206
(303)329-0202   FAX (303)329-9510

PROJECTS:
Private Residences: Chicago; New York;
Boca Raton, Florida; Denver, Aspen and
Vail, Colorado; Billings and Bozeman,
Montana; Palm Springs, California; and
Jedda, Saudi Arabia.

Commercial Work: Corporate offices,
financial institutions, restaurants, historic
restoration.

CREDENTIALS:
Montana State University, BS, MA
 interior design
ASID, Fellow, Professional Member
Marquis Who's Who in America
Barons Who's Who in Interior Design
24 regional and national awards

*ABOVE RIGHT: A parlor
designed to create an Old World
atmosphere combines finishes
from the 17th and 19th
centuries.*

*RIGHT: Architectural elements
and antiques emphasize the
intimacy of this dining room.*

*OPPOSITE: The rotunda gallery
in a European-styled manor
house deftly features Flemish,
French and Italian design
elements.*

LECZINSKI DESIGN ASSOCIATES

PUBLISHED IN:
Art in America
Interior Design
Architectural Digest
Designers Magazine
House Beautiful
Remodeling
Restaurant and Hotel Design
Sun/Coast Architect Builder
Colorado Homes and Lifestyles
Design Solution Journal

PHILOSOPHY:
Four commandments guide the artistic
endeavors of our projects: aesthetic
integrity, timelessness, clarity of design
and a sense of style.

*LEFT: Cathedral-like
interior architecture is the ideal
showcase for a dramatic mix of
classic furniture styles and
periods.*

*RIGHT: Juxtaposition of
materials and finishes brings
harmony to the open space of
this town home.*

*BELOW: A contrast in light
and texture, this cherry-detailed
library exudes warmth.*

LOVICK DESIGN

CORYNE LOVICK
11339 BURNHAM STREET
LOS ANGELES, CA 90049
(310)475-5781

PROJECTS:
Private Residences: California; South Hampton and White Plains, New York, NY; and Las Vegas.

Commercial Work: Gelare' on Sunset, Valerie Beverly Hills, KTLA, Fox, Linda Finer Skin Institute, Equity Marketing, Canon Insurance Co.; and private law offices.

CREDENTIALS:
Certified Interior Designer
Fashion Institute of Technology, New York
FIDM, Los Angeles
Epicurean Gala 1985

LOVICK DESIGN

LOWRANCE INTERIORS, INC.

JACK E. LOWRANCE
707 N. ALFRED
LOS ANGELES, CA 90069
(213)655-9713   FAX (213)655-0359

PROJECTS:
Private Residences: California; Hawaii; Montana; Oregon; Tennessee; Texas; Washington; New York City; Lake Tahoe, California; Japan; London; Mexico City; and Paris.

Commercial Work: Jimmy's Restaurant, Los Angeles, and "The Wilshire" Condominiums, Beverly Hills, California.

CREDENTIALS:
ASID, Allied Member
ISID (Jack Lowrance)
University of Texas
Texas Tech University
Wayland College

PUBLISHED IN:
Architectural Digest
Architectural Digest "The 100 Ad"
Bride's
California Home & Lifestyles
Homes International
House Beautiful
HG
Houston Chronicle
Los Angeles Times
Orange County Home & Garden
Southern Accents
Texas Homes
Unique Homes

LOWRANCE INTERIORS, INC.

PHILOSOPHY:
Our design style is contemporary with references to traditional. Contemporary design has a freshness that complements today's lifestyle, while historical design has a beauty and richness that can't be overlooked. We are as interested in the quality of the architecture as we are in the quality of the furnishings.

Our clients' needs, desires, wishes and dreams are of utmost importance in creating a living environment that reflects their personalities.

JUDITH LYNNE
P.O. BOX 4998
PALM SPRINGS, CA 92263
(619)324-7606   FAX (619)328-8190

RIGHT: Vibrant casual furniture complements an inspirational setting that straddles the line between indoor comfort and outdoor atmosphere.

BELOW: A classically appointed study in the 1995 Desert Showcase House offers a warm and welcoming retreat.

OPPOSITE: Sumptuous materials and striking accessories create a design whose hallmark is comfortable elegance.

JUDITH LYNNE
INTERIOR DESIGN

JUDITH LYNNE
INTERIOR DESIGN

PROJECTS:
Private Residences: California, Arizona, Illinois, Kansas and Switzerland.

Commercial Work: Hotels, country clubs and offices in California and Arizona.

CREDENTIALS:
ASID, Professional Member
1995 Desert Showcase House
Interior designer since 1977

PHILOSOPHY:
Good communication with clients, an understanding of their lifestyle, and an ability to express their design philosophy are the most important qualities of my work. I enjoy creating warm, gracious environments that meet the comfort and style requirements of my clients.
 I always try to craft a showcase for my clients' treasures, something that uniquely reflects their personality. The collaborative process should be fun and spirited, resulting in elegant surroundings of timeless quality in which you feel truly at home.

TOP: Cool blue fabric offers a soothing corner for reading and relaxation.

LEFT: Inspiring design elements breathe character into a functional space that's conducive to creativity and reflection.

LEFT: An understated flavoring of Oriental accents helps achieve a tranquil quality throughout this Indian Wells, California, home.

BELOW: A subtle palette mixes well with breezy linen fabrics, producing a sense of timelessness that's strengthened by the gold-framed art and mirror.

McCartney
& Thomas

ROBERT MCCARTNEY, ASID
1325 COAST BOULEVARD, SUITE B
LA JOLLA, CA 92037
(619)456-1659 FAX (619)456-1695

PROJECTS:
Private Residences: Rancho Santa Fe,
Fairbanks, La Jolla, San Diego, Orange
County, Los Angeles and San Francisco,
California; Detroit; Indianapolis; Atlanta;
and Shelter Island, New York.

Commercial Work:
Hotels, restaurants, corporate and
executive offices, condominium public
spaces, design of a private car museum
and furniture and product design.

CREDENTIALS:
ASID, Professional Member
California Certified Interior Designers
Excellence in Interior Design Award,
  ASID, four first-place awards
Designers Choice Award, ASID,
  five first-place awards
Published author of design articles
Local distinguished service citations

Robert McCartney, ASID:
Architecture and Design, Ireland

PUBLISHED IN:
Interiors
SDH/G Lifestyles
San Diego Magazine
Decorating & Style
Designers West
Ranch & Coast
Design Journal

PHILOSOPHY:
We take a creative approach to
integrating architecture and interiors. The
integrity of good design is determined
simply by what is appropriate.
   Architecture – what works well within
the bones of the space – is paramount.
Transition – the thread that weaves
through the design – provides unity and
flow while creating diversion and interest. Comfort, timelessness and quality
are mandatory. The successful design
that results should emanate a feeling,
not just a look.

*ABOVE LEFT: Arched
doorways and a generously
scaled hand-carved mirror
gracefully welcome visitors.*

*BELOW LEFT: A sensitive
balance among function, display
and comfort is achieved through
the careful manipulation of
architectural design, furnishings
and lighting.*

*OPPOSITE: Gentle colors and
form harmonize with the details
and quality of this formal space.
Notable features are the pale
apricot silk fabric, hand-carved
gilt mirrors and custom
limestone fireplace.*

McCartney & Thomas

LEFT: A gentleman's study crafted of cherry paneling serves as a quiet retreat for creative work.

BELOW: The unifying elements of subtle textures, quiet colors and soft lighting enhance the intimacy of this living room.

OPPOSITE: A comfortable, informal gathering place for the family - a good example of how design should embrace people, beauty and the activities of life.

McWHORTER
ASSOCIATES

BILL MCWHORTER, ASID
1041 1/2 S. GENESEE AVENUE
LOS ANGELES, CA 90019
(213)930-2113 FAX (213)936-4198

PROJECTS:
Private Residences: California; Bozeman, Montana; Aspen, Colorado; Hawaii; Texas; Ohio; Kentucky; New York; New Orleans; Wisconsin and Ireland.

Commercial Work: Corporate offices for Guess and Reebok, Spanish government offices, law offices, stores, restaurants and hospitality design.

CREDENTIALS:
ASID, Professional Member
AIA, Affiliate Member
Pasadena Showcase House of Design, 1992-95
Little Company of Mary Showcase House of Design, 1992, 1994
Desert Showcase House (Eisenhower Medical Center), 1995
Beastly Ball, fund-raiser for Los Angeles Zoo, 1995
S.M. Hexter, Interior of the Year Award
Better Homes & Gardens Home Improvement Contest, first place
Ohio State University, B.F.A.

PUBLISHED IN:
Architectural Digest
Cincinnati Magazine
Designers West
House & Garden
House Beautiful
Interior Design
La Jolla Magazine
Palm Springs Life
San Diego Magazine

PHILOSOPHY:
I approach each project with a sense of adventure and wit, trying always to pique the imagination of my clients by introducing them to concepts they hadn't considered.

An interior should be beautiful, comfortable and practical, while reflecting the personality of clients within a framework of taste, style and panache. Scale, proportion, color, lighting and eclecticism are keys to my work.

Quite often, I design furnishings, lighting fixtures and fabrics to enhance rooms. Interesting architectural details are the backbone of compelling interiors. If they don't exist, I create them.

Through collaborative relationships with my clients, my interiors are romantic, classic, timeless ... and innovative. And since I'm not locked into a particular style or period, they are also singular, exciting and unexpected.

LEFT: The beaded African table, contemporary art, Chinese pot and custom Arts and Crafts-inspired lamp table are eclectic counterpoints to the Baronial English-style architecture of this rathskeller. Hand-glazed fir green walls elegantly complement the limestone floor, stone arches and dark wood-beamed ceiling.

ABOVE: In a room overlooking the ocean, jade and celadon greens mixed with sand and bleached neutral tones echo the outdoors. Fishtail palm trees in Raku pots, massive agave attenuata on a giant faux stone coffee table, comfortably generous upholstery and a custom rug with king-size checkerboard are in scale to the room's proportions. An antique Chinese camphorwood cabinet anchors the room and lends ancient-world tone.

ABOVE OPPOSITE: Dark ceiling beams, a wood floor and an antique French credenza contrast with the yellow damask wall upholstery, thick ivory chenille fabric and plaster relief ceiling. The window and door moldings are painted green faux marble. Natural grass window blinds and a custom hand-painted sisal and broadloom rug are other unexpected elements.

BELOW OPPOSITE: A feeling of Tuscany is evoked in this dining room in a desert house. The terra cotta-colored wall drapery with its scrubbed finish resembling weathered Italian walls gives softness and texture, while the seven-foot stone and marble table, stone planters, antique priests' vestment chest and rusted-iron chandelier add scale. The painting pays homage to Michelangelo.

MOORE/MURRAY ASSOCIATES

PATRICIA MURRAY
8687 MELROSE AVENUE, SUITE M46
LOS ANGELES, CA 90069
(310)289-2940 FAX (310)289-2944

PROJECTS:
Private Residences: Santa Monica and
Los Angeles, California; and Vancouver,
British Columbia.

CREDENTIALS:
AIA, Member
CCIDC, certification
IIDA, Professional Member
Fashion Institute of Design and
 Merchandising, Los Angeles (A.A.
 interior design)
Southern California Institute of
 Architecture, Santa Monica (B.A.
 architecture)
Southern California Institute of
 Architecture, Switzerland (bachelor of
 architecture)
City of West Hollywood's Recommended
 Architects List
Divine Design '94 and '95 Showcase
 Designer

PUBLISHED IN:
Los Angeles Times Magazine
Los Angeles Style
Audio Visual Magazine
People
In Style
Western Living

PHILOSOPHY:
Initially, I prefer to present a range of
design options that meet the needs and
budget of my client. I encourage clients
to participate in the design process,
and I try to incorporate their personalities
as much as possible. My education
and experience in both interior and
architectural design allow me to integrate
all aspects of design and create a single
work of art.

*LEFT: A craftsman home built
in Vancouver in 1913 is updated
with a new staircase and an
abundance of light.*

*ABOVE OPPOSITE: An
existing bedroom in Los Angeles
is expanded and refinished to
accommodate a sitting area. A
television pops up from the
maple table adjacent to the
custom sofa.*

*BELOW OPPOSITE: A new
kitchen in Santa Monica reflects
the functional requirements and
personal style of its owners.*

NANCY MULLAN,
ASID, CKD

NDM KITCHENS INC.
204 E. 77TH ST.
NEW YORK, NY 10021
(212)628-4629   FAX (212)628-6738

PROJECTS:
Private Residences: New York City and the Hamptons, New York; Greenwich, Connecticut; Philadelphia; Sun Valley, Idaho; Los Angeles; and the Bahamas.

CREDENTIALS:
ASID, professional member
NCIDQ certified
Certified Kitchen Designer
Governor CKD Society
National Kitchen & Bath Association
  member
Kips Bay Showhouse, 1992, 1995
Southampton Showhouse, 1988, 1993
Greenwich Showhouse, 1991

PUBLISHED IN:
Country Living (cover)
House Beautiful (cover)
House Beautiful Kitchens & Baths
  (cover)
Interior Design Magazine
Woman's Day
Who's Who in Interior Design
New York Times
Washington Post

PHILOSOPHY:
The key to good interior design is comfort - physical comfort, of course, but also visual and emotional comfort. Regardless of its style, a space should make us feel good and want to stay there. I try to follow the advice of William Morris: "Have nothing in your houses that you do not know to be useful or believe to be beautiful."

BELOW: Seascape murals, pickled floors and five shades of gray paint create an ethereal backdrop for entertaining. Reprinted by permission from House Beautiful, *copyright © September 1995. The Hearst Corporation. All rights reserved. Photographer, Richard Felber.*

LEFT: This fully functional home office is tucked into the corner of a family room. The monitor is recessed into the wall, the printer is closeted underneath, the computer and disks are in the cabinet on the right, and the keyboard and mouse pad fold into the drawer. Everything is instantly accessible - and easily concealed.

BELOW: Featured on the September '95 cover of House Beautiful, *this cheerful kitchen and family room are furnished for flexibility. Antiqued cabinets conceal the refrigerator (left background). Reprinted by permission from* House Beautiful, *copyright © September 1995. The Hearst Corporation. All rights reserved. Photographer, Richard Felber.*

PAT STOTLER INTERIORS INC.

PATRICIA S. STOTLER
110 CORAL CAY DRIVE
PALM BEACH GARDENS, FL 33418
(407)627-0527   FAX (407)626-7015

PROJECTS:
Private Residences: South Florida,
Cincinnati and Houston.

CREDENTIALS:
Westchester College, B.S.
Syracuse University, M.S.
Lighthouse Gallery Showcase Houses,
  1991-92

PUBLISHED IN:
100 Designers' Favorite Rooms
Palm Beach Illustrated
Focus Magazine
Miami Herald
Indian River Pictorial
Palm Beach Post
Palm Beach County Visitors Guide
Showcase of Interior Design,
  Southern Editions I and II
Treasure Coast Magazine
Interior Design Library of Dining Rooms
Interior Designers' Showcase of Color
Florida Design

PHILOSOPHY:
Creating beautiful surroundings is an
exhilarating experience. I love watching
rooms evolve throughout the design
process, from initial selection of fine
fabrics and furnishings to final
installation. The most rewarding aspect
of any project occurs when I see my
clients' expressions as they inspect every
detail of their new environment.

*LEFT: Brightly colored plaid
fabric and a handcrafted
chandelier complement light
wood furnishings in an airy
breakfast room.*

*BELOW: Detailed molding
on the honey-tone cabinetry is
repeated on the custom-built
desk. Leather chairs, a green
ultra-suede sofa and a lamp
built around an Old World globe
add to the air of sophistication.*

*OPPOSITE: Vanilla-colored silk
sofas and down-filled chairs face
an iron cocktail table displaying
brushed pewter candlesticks and
an Italian porcelain swan.*

PAT STOTLER INTERIORS INC.

RIGHT: Silk fabrics in tones of black and beige, silver-leaf lamps and soothing artwork establish a mood of relaxed elegance.

BELOW: Comfortable seating and tapestry fabrics create an environment of casual living enhanced further by the rusty-red textured coffee table. Note how honey tones and washed wood mix in the entertainment center.

OPPOSITE: Custom crackle-finished chairs and a stone-base table add an air of Old World elegance to a richly decorated dining room. Note also the handcrafted chandelier and the large mirror with a hand-carved wood frame.

FRANK K.
PENNINO &
ASSOCIATES

FRANK K. PENNINO
8654 HOLLOWAY PLAZA DRIVE
LOS ANGELES, CA 90069
(310)657-8847 FAX (310)657-0227

CREDENTIALS:
Instructor UCLA Advanced Residential
  Seminars and Extension Program
Architectural Digest 100 Finest Designers
  in the World, 1990,1995

PUBLISHED IN:
Architectural Digest
House & Garden
House Beautiful
Los Angeles Magazine
Los Angeles Times

PHILOSOPHY:
For 25 years, our firm has provided
beautiful environments to complement
the unique and diverse personalities of
our clients.

Although we prefer a historical
reference point, we do not have a signa-
ture style. Each project evolves from the
needs of the client and the inspiration
from the house itself.

Most of our work is residential, though
we have designed many corporate headquarters for companies that demand a
distinctive design statement.

Our company has the honor of being
included in both editions of
"Architectural Digest 100 Finest
Designers in the World," and many of
our projects have been featured in
national and international publications.

*BELOW: An informal back-
ground complements a wonderful
collection of Indian art in this
corporate dining room.*

ABOVE: Hand woven textiles and Indian artifacts enrich this reception area for a screening room.

FRANK K. PENNINO & ASSOCIATES

ABOVE: The contemporary architecture in this Los Angeles pied-a-terre is softened through the use of rich woods, indirect lighting and designs from the '30s.

ABOVE: A muted aubusson
carpet, soft colors and traditional
French furnishings create the
European feeling desired by the
young actress who owns this
Beverly Hills apartment.

POET DESIGN COMPANY

CAROL POET
540 NORTH SAN VICENTE BLVD.
WEST HOLLYWOOD, CA 90048
(310)854-6100   FAX (310)652-2817

PROJECTS:
Private Residences: Don Bellisario, Leslie Belzberg, Kathleen Brown & Van Gordon Sauter, Steve Dontanville, Richard Dreyfuss, Judy & Peter Fonda, Gary David Goldberg & Diana Meehan (Los Angeles, Malibu & Vermont), Paula Holt, Gale Anne Hurd, Judith Parker & John Peaslee, RuPaul, Sid & Lorraine Sheinberg, Richard Simmons, Rita & Haskell Wexler, Strauss Zelnick & Wendy Belzberg, (Los Angeles and New York).

Commercial Work: Bank of Los Angeles, Katz Medical Building, First Pacific Bank, Long Beach Savings & Loan (Beverly Hills), Pacific Motion Pictures (Los Angeles), Westwood Savings & Loan, Chartoff/Winkler Productions, Jeff Wald offices, Slimmons Gym, Sheinbergs Bubble Factory.

CREDENTIALS:
Licensed interior designer
International Interior Design Association
NCIDQ Certified
International Society of Interior
   Designers, board member
Los Angeles County Museum of Art,
   1987 Art & Architecture Tour
Bel-Air Design House, 1992
Palos Verdes Design House, 1993
Divine Design 1995
Television production design

OPPOSITE: Partially underground, this guest room used to be a dark, cold and dank storage space. The walls were sealed, padded and upholstered to create warmth and coziness. Sophisticated lighting sidesteps the problem presented by one small window and helps turn the space into a romantic hideaway.

RIGHT: Because it was in the first branch of a new banking institution, this lobby was designed within a limited budget. Inexpensive materials don't distract from the sophisticated post-modern style.

BELOW: This retreat leading to a private patio off a master suite offers several lifestyle options – reading in the custom-designed boar hide chair and ottoman, writing at the original Deco desk, or lounging on a woven leather window bench.

J. POWELL &
ASSOCIATES, INC.

JIM POWELL
210 OFFERSON ROAD
P.O. BOX 1641
AVON, CO 81620
(970)845-7731   FAX (970)845-8903

PROJECTS:
Private Residences: Vail, Beaver Creek
and Denver, Colorado; Chicago; Houston;
Tulsa; New York; and Kansas City,
Missouri.

Commercial Work: Hotel and hospitality,
medical and dental facilities, advertising
and executive offices.

CREDENTIALS:
Oklahoma State University, B.S.
  interior design
Practicing interior designer since 1977
Best of Beaver Creek home tours

PHILOSOPHY:
The majestic beauty of the Rocky
Mountains provides a colorful palette for
many of our regional interiors. Our goal
is to create a home that fulfills our
clients' needs and brings reality to their
dreams.

*ABOVE LEFT: The mixing of an
antique hutch and accessories
with a reproduction dining table
and chairs creates a cozy area
for casual or formal dining.*

*LEFT: A unique iron
bed and bench combine with
reproduction wood furnishings
and muted florals to provide an
interesting, yet relaxing, master
bedroom suite.*

*OPPOSITE: Casual elegance
dominates this mountain home
situated on the side of a ski
slope. Warm tones on the faux
painted walls and rich cherry
trim, floors and beams provide
a dramatic backdrop for the
country French furnishings and
decorative accessories.*

J. Powell &
Associates, Inc.

RIGHT: Blue pearl granite is used throughout this Chicago high-rise, which offers a view of Lake Michigan and the city's skyline. Black glass soffits are used to conceal electronic screens and down lights. The jewel tones of the custom area rug provide dramatic color and texture for this contemporary setting.

BELOW: Maple and granite inlaid into the oak floor enhance a bed of bird's-eye maple and cherry veneer. Silk-upholstered walls allow the cityscape to provide most of the artwork.

OPPOSITE: This dramatic entry showcases a Patricia Baez glass sculpture. Stainless steel divides the faux finished walls and forms the channel for the vault lighting.

P.T.M. Interiors
Unlimited
Designs

CREDENTIALS:
Feng Shui, Master B.T.B.
ASID, Accredited Associate Member
International Interior Design Association
American Center for Design
Institute of Business Designers
Color Marketing Group
Association for International Color
  Directions

PUBLISHED IN:
Showcase of Interior Design
Who's Who in Interior Design, 1992-94
Who's Who of the Asian Pacific Rim
100 Designers' Favorite Rooms
Interior Designers' Showcase of Color
Among others

PHILOSOPHY:
I focus on the lifestyle needs of my clients and combine traditional design elements with current ideas to create an aesthetic balance in their home or work space.

Design is a reflection of life. I constantly develop new services and products to meet the needs of my clients.

CAROL MELTZER
TURTLE BAY TOWERS
310 EAST 46TH ST., STE. 16-L
NEW YORK, NY 10017
(212)681-9881   FAX (212)681-9877

PROJECTS:
Private Residences and Commercial Work: New York; Palm Springs and Los Angeles, California; Palm Beach, Florida; Ontario, Canada; Tokyo and Osaka, Japan; and London.

ABOVE: The use of round and square shapes, the curve of the natural marble, and the incorporation of mirrors, copper and wood are among the Feng Shui design elements that bring energy to this powder room.

LEFT: Minimal use of accessories emphasizes the sharp simplicity of this modern kitchen. Classic black tones contrast with bird's eye maple cabinetry to strengthen the room's sense of refined elegance. Note how the convex light fixture helps dramatize the room's height.

OPPOSITE: This contemporary house with views of the Atlantic Ocean integrates all the principles of Feng Shui, the ancient Chinese discipline of creating maximum harmony and energy in one's life through the use of shapes, colors and textures.

JUSTINE RINGLIEN, ASID
96 RIDGEVIEW DRIVE
ATHERTON, CA 94027
(415)233-0330   FAX (415)854-7733

PROJECTS:
Private Residences: California and
Washington.

Commercial Work: Cliff House
Restaurant, San Francisco; Spinnaker
Restaurant, Sausalito, California; Cantina
Restaurants, Marin County, California;
Vintage House Restaurants; MV
Catamaran Ferry and MV Dolphin Ferry,
Crowley Corp.; and clubhouses and
condominiums in California.

CREDENTIALS:
ASID, Professional Member since 1970
ASID Northern California Vice President,
 1989-91
ASID Speakers Bureau
ASID Design Excellence Award,
 Hospitality, 1991
Belvedere, California House Tour,
 1985-87
Napa Designers' Showcase, 1989
Atherton Family Services House Tour,
 1994
CCIDC, 1994
Designers on Parade Tribute

PUBLISHED IN:
San Francisco Chronicle
San Francisco Examiner
Sacramento Bee
Showplace Square Today
Santa Rosa Business Journal
Sunset
Better Homes & Gardens
Interiors
In Marin
Designers West

*RIGHT: An antique Chinese
polychrome horse and African
accessories introduce an
unusual touch to this home
office.*

*OPPOSITE: Antique furnishings
and accessories bring a sense of
timelessness to this master
suite.*

JUSTINE RINGLIEN INTERIORS

PHILOSOPHY:
Successful interior design depends on a partnership between designer and client. Much of my work departs from the very traditional and formal by stressing simple forms, contrasting textures, proportion and scale. I also emphasize lighting and flow between interior and exterior spaces. My goal is to create environments that are timeless, appropriate and suited to the client's lifestyle.

OPPOSITE, TOP LEFT: The homeowner's collection of antique brass blends beautifully with the stainless steel appliances and washed oak cabinetry.

OPPOSITE, TOP RIGHT: Custom dinnerware, glassware and tableware grace a richly orchestrated space.

OPPOSITE: Custom furniture and Moroccan pottery help integrate this exterior setting with the home's interior style.

TOP LEFT: Contemporary furnishings and antique artifacts mix easily here. The custom dining chairs are slipcovered, allowing the room to be changed at a whim.

LEFT: Serene shades of white create tranquility in this pool house retreat.

RŌ-CHE-ÉT
DESIGNS

LEO ROCHETTE III
1441 ROSE VILLA STREET
PASADENA, CA 91106
(818)585-8227

PROJECTS:
Private Residences: Beverly Hills, Bel-Air, Pacific Palisades, Pasadena, San Marino, Westlake, Montecito, Newport Beach and San Francisco, California; Phoenix; Ocala and Daytona Beach, Florida; and Indonesia.

Commercial Work: Executive offices and hospitality facilities in California.

CREDENTIALS:
The Fashion Institute of Design & Merchandising
Recipient of The Fashion Institute of Design & Merchandising Scholarship, 1987
1994 Pasadena Showcase House of Design
1995 Pasadena Showcase House of Design
Pasadena Symphony Association Benefit Committee
Advisory Board of PLANET HOPE

PUBLISHED IN:
Bon Appetit
Southern California Home & Garden
"Walker Zanger" national advertisements
Contemporary Stone Design
Hospitality Design
Town & Country
Los Angeles Times

PHILOSOPHY:
Clients call on a designer to interpret style. I approach projects in an effort to define that style, to educate clients, and to refine their desires.

As an architectural interior designer, there's great satisfaction in bringing an entire project together from start to finish, whether dealing with new construction or historic renovations.

Knowing how to work within a client's budget to achieve the highest impact is my main focus. The most rewarding aspect of my work is being absorbed by a client's excitement when a project is complete.

ABOVE OPPOSITE: An 18th century neoclassical bench complements this vanity. The octagonal area is flanked by four mirrored doors leading to walk-in closets. A custom inlaid marble medallion contributes subtle detail throughout.

BELOW OPPOSITE: An 18th century Russian chandelier enhances the vanity area of this master bath suite, which also serves as a foyer into the master bedroom. A pair of custom etched doors drawn by the designer are in the foreground.

LEFT: Hand-painted porcelain bowls, gold-plated fixtures and Italian marble establish the rich style of the individual pullmans.

BELOW: This master bath suite, of entirely new construction, is flanked by a pair of neoclassical cabinets that serve as pullmans. Fluted columns frame the custom etched glass window drawn by the designer. French limestone of beaumaniere and buffon comes together to create the floor pattern throughout.

RonAllen Enterprises

PROJECTS:
Private Residences: Beverly Hills, Century City, Palm Springs and Pacific Palisades, California; Palm Beach, Florida; New York; Las Vegas; England; and France.

Commercial Work:
Executive law offices in Beverly Hills and Century City, California; executive office in New York; and designs for Red Onion and Tampico Tillie restaurants in California.

CREDENTIALS:
Woodbury College
Pasadena Showcase House of Design, 1990, 1991
ISID Showcase Hancock Park, 1987
Chaplin DeMille Design House, 1989
ASID, Allied Member
IIDA, Member
ISID, President, 1991, 1993

RON HUDSON, ALLIED ASID, IIDA
1039 SWARTHMORE AVENUE
PACIFIC PALISADES, CA 90272
(310)459-7039   FAX (310)459-2760

BELOW: This formal entry features a floor of limestone, sandstone and marble, along with a pair of Louis XVI armchairs and matching hand-carved, gilded consoles. Note how the silk dynasty wall covering sets off the Oriental art.

OPPOSITE: A dramatic use of columns enhances the seating area and piano beyond.

RonAllen
Enterprises

PUBLISHED IN:
Designers West
Window Fashions
Pasadena Showcase
California Homes & Lifestyles
Limited Editions Great Estates, 1989

PHILOSOPHY:
The relationship between client and designer is the most important aspect of interior design. In all my work, I seek to offer functional solutions that respect the personal style and taste of my clients.

The client's wish list dominates my thoughts at the start of any project. Light, color, texture and scale all reflect the client's lifestyle. Unity with flow and diversion with interest are the threads that should weave through a home. Comfort, even in the most formal areas, is mandatory.

BELOW: A blend of French and English furniture mixes with Oriental art to achieve an international flavor. The antique English gilded chairs with Egyptian arms are from Therien & Co.

ABOVE OPPOSITE: A silk dynasty wall covering and a hand-painted border accent Egyptian art in this comfortable media room. The custom-designed mantel adds warmth.

BELOW OPPOSITE: Rich cherry paneling showcases an extensive library and collection of antique instruments.

PENELOPE ROZIS

PENELOPE ROZIS
720 PINE STREET
SAN FRANCISCO, CA 94108
(415) 387-8844   FAX (415) 362-8879

PROJECTS:
Private Residences: San Francisco, Brentwood, Beverly Hills, Hillsborough, Napa Valley and Santa Barbara, California; Sun Valley, Idaho; Chicago; and Grosse Pointe, Michigan.

Commercial Work:
San Francisco and Los Angeles.

CREDENTIALS:
University of Michigan
Skidmore, Owings & Merrill
The Pfister Partnership

PHILOSOPHY:
Whether contemporary or classic, a good interior is timeless, comfortable and functional, while reflecting the taste of the owner.

LEFT: Gold details and dark wood provide a counterpoint to the classical scenes in the upholstered walls and drapery.

BELOW: Custom designed furniture and antique oriental rugs are the key elements in this high rise executive office.

OPPOSITE: A light background and pastel palette combine with contemporary furniture and antiques to complement an extraordinary art collection.

SAMANTHA COLE
1319 HOWARD AVENUE
BURLINGAME, CA 94010
(415)344-5400 FAX (415)344-5697

PROJECTS:
Private Residences: San Francisco,
Hillsborough, Atherton, Woodside,
Tiburon, Lafayette, Danville and Los
Angeles, California; Sun Valley, Idaho;
Boca Raton, Florida; and New York City.

CREDENTIALS:
ASID, Allied Member
California State University, B.A.
 art history and design
San Francisco Symphony Showhouse,
 1992
Coyote Point Museum Showhouse, 1993
ASID Showhouse, 1994
American Cancer Society Showhouse,
 1994, 1995

PUBLISHED IN:
House Beautiful
Country Home
Accessory Magazine
San Francisco Chronicle
Gentry
Designers Illustrated

PHILOSOPHY:
We work closely with clients to create
homes that are inviting and timelessly
elegant, and which always reflect our
clients' taste, personality, and lifestyle.

SAMANTHA COLE

OPPOSITE: A charming French folly, this breakfast room was designed to be a sunny, whimsical pavilion. The chinoiserie lantern and playful mural characters inspire a lighthearted morning.

RIGHT: A warm, cozy cocoon in which to unwind at the end of a long day, this sitting room features a stately library and a comfortably elegant European sofa that invites private conversation.

BELOW: Custom valances with an awning effect evoke thoughts of dining alfresco, while the furnishings set the mood for sumptuously comfortable dining.

SISTINE INTERIORS

SHARON SISTINE ASID, IIDA, CID
1359 N. BEVERLY DRIVE
BEVERLY HILLS, CA 90210
(310)246-1888   FAX (310)246-1889

PROJECTS:
Private Residences: Nationwide interior and exterior design.

CREDENTIALS:
ASID, Professional Member
IIDA, Professional Member
IIDA, Board of Directors,
VP/Communication and Membership, Southern California
Certified Interior Designer, California
University of Minnesota, B.S.
New York School of Interior Design

Bloomingdale's Interior Design Department, New York City
Interior Design Stylist for celebrity home photography
ASID Desert Showcase House of Design, 1995
Pasadena Showcase House of Design, 1995
Pasadena Showcase House of Design, 1996
Assistance League Showcase House, 1995
Divine Design, 1995
ISID Showcase House, 1992

BELOW: Antique garden accessories and simple furnishings come together in a rustic patio retreat.

OPPOSITE: The golden glow of the late afternoon sun and the warmth of a roaring fire enhance an inviting lakeside veranda furnished with antique Anglo Indian pieces.

SISTINE INTERIORS

PUBLISHED IN:
House & Garden
Designers West
Palm Springs Life
Country Sampler
Sunset Books
Valley Magazine
Syndicated newspapers and
   trade journals

PHILOSOPHY:
My goal is to enrich the lives of my clients by creating intensely personal homes that are friendly and open-hearted, with the romance of the good life woven throughout.

LEFT: Set against richly "leathered" walls are an antique Dutch East Indian captain's chest and a classic brass architectural mirror.

BELOW: The designer's home, a restored 1920s Mediterranean hideaway, features sandblasted ceilings, tile floors and eclectic collectibles.

OPPOSITE: Created for the 1995 Pasadena Showcase House of Design, this aristocratic, yet friendly, young gentleman's bedroom is furnished with heirloom pieces and touches of whimsy, including a much-loved teddy bear.

THURSTON
KITCHEN & BATH

STEPHEN T. MCDONALD
2920 EAST SIXTH AVE.
DENVER, CO 80206
(303)399-4564   (303)333-4406

LEFT: Traditional lines accent classic cabinet design in medium stain on butternut. The countertops are venziano granite. Vail, Colorado.

BELOW: Here, sleek design is accented with a Southwestern flair. The older cabinets feature an autumn red heirloom finish. Reflections of light bounce from the absolute black granite tile countertops. Eagle, Colorado.

ABOVE: Large open-cut log walls create a feeling of permanence and the West. The interior boasts a comfortable feel, echoed within the design of the kitchen. The cabinets are clear vertical grain fir in a natural finish. Unique marble-top island and AGA range enhance the function and style. Telluride, Colorado.

RIGHT: This spacious kitchen makes it easy to prepare food and accommodate large gatherings. The stainless steel hood and Viking range incorporate commercial touches. Vail, Colorado.

JASON TITUS
INTERIORS

JASON TITUS, ASID
16 TECHNOLOGY DRIVE, #137
IRVINE, CA 92718
(714)753-1176   FAX (714)453-0375

PROJECTS:
Private Residences: La Jolla, San Diego, Newport Beach, Newport Coast, Laguna Beach, Palm Springs, Palm Desert, Glendale, Pasadena, Riverside, Berkeley and Napa, California.

Commercial Work: Restaurants, clubs, ships, hotels, retail shops, law, medical and dental offices.

CREDENTIALS:
ASID, Professional Member
California Certified Interior Designer
University of Oregon, B.A., architecture
Interior design instructor in professional
   interior design programs
Contributing writer for "By Design" in
   Los Angeles Times
Orange County Philharmonic House of
   Design, 1991, 1992, 1993, 1995

PUBLISHED IN:
Better Homes & Gardens Decorating
Orange County House & Garden
Orange Coast Magazine
Household
Los Angeles Times
Orange County Register

OPPOSITE ABOVE: Time-honored family furnishings and a custom daybed designed by Jason Titus Interiors highlight this English-style library, which doubles as a guest room.

OPPOSITE: This contemporary guest room features faux parchment paneled walls, a custom bookcase and a bedside table designed by Jason Titus Interiors. The paintings of local landscapes are by a Southern California artist.

LEFT: French antiques, Oriental porcelain and old brass fill this high-ceiling library, an ideal spot for reading, writing or quiet conversation.

PHILOSOPHY:
Established in 1977, Jason Titus Interiors is known for high quality commercial and residential work. Each project is carefully developed to address the needs of the client, the existing architecture and the interior detailing.

Design solutions include custom cabinets, furniture, special art and artifacts, lighting layouts and reconstruction ideas. Quality starts with the design concept and ends with a beautifully executed interior.

TOMAR LAMPERT
ASSOCIATES

STEPHEN TOMAR, ASID
STUART LAMPERT
8900 MELROSE AVENUE, SUITE 202
LOS ANGELES, CA 90069
(310)271-4299   FAX (310)271-1569

PROJECTS:
Private Residences: Los Angeles, Beverly Hills, Malibu, San Diego and Rancho Sante Fe, California; Palm Beach and Miami Beach, Florida; Philadelphia; New York; Sun Valley, Idaho and Las Vegas.

Commercial Work: Hotels, restaurants, retail space and executive offices.

PUBLISHED IN:
Architectural Digest
House Beautiful
L.A. Magazine
Hollywood Reporter
Designer West
Angeles Magazine

PHILOSOPHY:
A home is the most personal expression of one's self. We create each room so that it is a reflection of our client's taste and lifestyle. A good designer is a master of interpretation, able to extract from clients a vision of their completed home.

By emphasizing substance, style and tradition over trends, our homes have a timeless quality. We begin each project by assessing the house from the outside in, paying particular attention to the architecture to determine how the interiors can be used to their best advantage. We may design furniture, cabinetry or custom lighting, or even reconstruct an entire space, to achieve the intended appearance and function of a room.

Our homes have one thing in common - attention to detail. Often, it is the smallest components of a house that make it unique and enduring.

ABOVE: Inspired by Moroccan style, this refined library offers mahogany paneling with turned mahogany columns.

ABOVE OPPOSITE: This traditional drawing room features a 17th century aubusson rug, coffered ceilings and a mix of antique and classic furnishings.

BELOW OPPOSITE: Soaring 20-foot ceilings, traditional furnishings and a metallic grasscloth wall covering are among the dramatic touches in this living room.

TOMAR LAMPERT ASSOCIATES

RIGHT: Located in a Los Angeles penthouse, this kitchen and adjacent living space redefine country style for the '90s.

BELOW: Vibrant crayon colors electrify this living room, helping to brighten a home situated in a canyon.

ABOVE OPPOSITE: Cherubs float above the bed and gold leaf cornices adorn each window in a bedroom fit for royalty.

BELOW OPPOSITE Soft, warm colors and classic furnishings evoke serenity.

Ron Wilson
Designer

RON WILSON
1235 TOWER ROAD
BEVERLY HILLS, CA 90210
(310)276-0666   FAX (310)276-7291

PROJECTS:
Private residences, celebrity homes, banks and corporate offices world wide.

PUBLISHED IN:
Architectural Digest
House and Garden
Allure
House Beautiful
People
Antique Monthly

PHILOSOPHY:
Ron Wilson is one of the country's foremost interior designers, known for incorporating a feeling of quiet authority and taste while carefully considering the client's comfort and living requirements. His versatility, discretion and sense of quality continue to be in demand among a wealthy and celebrated circle of clients.

LEFT: This turreted dining room features carved Venetian chairs and a large chandelier with sandblasted crystals.

BELOW: Draped chairs and a hand-wrought, unwired iron chandelier with candles are among the unique features in this dramatic dining room.

OPPOSITE: An antique iron chandelier presides over a dining table with antique French chairs in this oval morning room.

RON WILSON
DESIGNER

RIGHT: A magnificent master bedroom achieves formal balance with architectural details like Tuscan columns, panel molding and a custom tray ceiling.

BELOW: Beige chenille upholstery and iron floor lamps with parchment shades contribute to the casual elegance of a Malibu living room.

OPPOSITE: A limestone fireplace and inviting over-stuffed furniture complement the neutral background in a Bel-Air living room.

NORM WOGAN
DESIGN

NORM WOGAN
P.O. BOX 691433
LOS ANGELES, CA 90069
(213)782-8001   FAX (213)782-8003

PROJECTS:
Private Residences: Los Angeles and
Malibu, California.

PUBLISHED IN:
Custom Home Magazine
Interior Designers' Showcase of Color

OPPOSITE TOP: Inviting water and lush plants frame an oasis of distinctive design.

OPPOSITE BOTTOM: In the Malibu residence of Stan Herman, elegant interior design merges effortlessly with the natural beauty of the outdoors.

ABOVE: A stone wall and floor provide the backdrop for a collection of naturally eclectic accessories.

NORM WOGAN
DESIGN

PHILOSOPHY:
I enjoy creating living spaces that engage all the senses and effortlessly draw the eye from one aspect of the environment to the next.

Working with a home's existing architecture is the basis of interior design.

Equally as important is the ability to integrate personal antiques or art into the design scheme so the home clearly represents the client's sensibilities and taste. A strong working relationship depends on listening to clients and expressing a consistent interpretation of their needs.

BELOW: An ornate chandelier and mirror frame are among the elegant counterpoints in a room that seems to flow effortlessly outside.

LEFT: Natural materials combine with casual accents that occasionally border on the rustic to give this living space a style that's easy to appreciate.

BELOW: Bookshelves, plants and accessories provide splashes of color in a bedroom grounded in warm, natural tones.

C.M. WRIGHT INC.

CRAIG WRIGHT
700 N. LA CIENEGA BLVD.
LOS ANGELES, CA 90069
(310)657-7655 FAX (310)657-4440

PROJECTS:
Private Residences: Los Angeles; San Francisco; New York; Santa Fe, New Mexico; Aspen, Colo.; Jackson Hole, Wyo.; Canada; Spain; France; and Switzerland.

CREDENTIALS:
Two decades experience in design and architecture
Founded own design firm in 1980

PUBLISHED IN:
Architectural Digest
House & Garden
Town & Country
Interior Design
Ad International
AD 100

ABOVE: *The play of contemporary furniture in a traditional environment creates a pleasing interior.*

OPPOSITE: *Movable curtains divide space for different functions in this office. Note the contemporary granite table and Italian neoclassical painted furniture. Faux fresco walls add to the impression of a space in transition.*

C.M. Wright Inc.

PHILOSOPHY:
My work is classical, somewhat traditional, bordering on the extravagant – but with boundaries. I focus on strong architectural backgrounds and prefer using unusual off-tone colors. My rooms are based on counterpoint, with thought-provoking elements that don't reveal themselves instantly.

I prefer using objects and furniture that have passed the test of time, often creating rooms which seem timeless, yet original. Also, I enjoy being involved in the initial architectural planning because this can save much time and expense.

BELOW: A combination of disparate elements works in graceful harmony.

OPPOSITE: The great room in a Spanish revival house uses no color, allowing exotic furniture to appear as sculpture against white walls.

BELOW OPPOSITE: Chinese antiquities provide a counterpoint to crisp, fresh furnishings.

B. JORDAN
YOUNG, INC.

BETTYE JORDAN YOUNG
8570 HILLSIDE AVENUE
LOS ANGELES, CA 90069
(213)650-0101 FAX (213)650-0835

PROJECTS:
Private Residences and Commercial
Work: New York and Southampton;
Atlanta; Dallas; Palm Beach; Los
Angeles; and London.

CREDENTIALS:
Georgia State University, B.F.A.
Guest lecturer and critic
Savannah College of Arts & Design
Parsons School of Design
Who's Who in Interior Design

PUBLISHED IN:
Architectural Digest
Interiors
Interior Design
Kateigaho

*BELOW: A rhythm is
established through the careful
synthesis of the building
structure and the furniture
selection.*

*OPPOSITE: Like a favorite piece
of music, good design is never
tiring.*

B. JORDAN YOUNG, INC.

ABOVE: The clients wished to use restraint in accommodating their needs without losing sight of the extraordinary architecture.

RIGHT: This sumptuous living room is part of a Fifth Avenue apartment that consists of four rooms from what was formerly one of New York's finest private residences. It's now used for short stays in the city and business entertaining.

LEFT: Terminating a progression of fin de siecle rooms, the master bedroom in this apartment exudes an aura of ease.

BELOW: A palette of patinated colors calms a fluctuating light from the west wall during the day and evens out the limited light sources in the evening.

SARA ZOOK
DESIGNS, LTD.

SARA ZOOK, ASID
2001-A YOUNGFIELD STREET
GOLDEN, CO 80401
(303)237-4544 FAX (303)237-1647

BELOW: Strong architectural details in the fireplace and windows set the mood for this comfortable living room. Tiered gardens of flowers reflect the soft palette inside, while walnut floors underscore the soft warmth of the pastel Oriental rugs and Chinese porcelains.

ABOVE: Set amid pines and a nearby stream, this country bedroom serves as a respite on a thousand-acre mountain ranch in Colorado. The maple canopy bed takes advantage of the soaring vaulted ceiling and complements the light woods used on the balcony.

PROJECTS:
Private Residences: Denver, Cherry Hills, Boulder, Evergreen, Genessee, Aspen and Vail, Colorado; Chicago; Atlanta; Minneapolis; Green Lake, Wisconsin; Laguna Niguel, California; Scottsdale and Tucson, Arizona.

Commercial Work: Corporate offices, hospitality facilities, trade showrooms, resorts, restaurants and retail stores.

CREDENTIALS:
ASID, Past Secretary, Illinois Chapter
ASID, Board of Directors,
 Colorado Chapter
Denver Symphony Guild Showhouses
University of Colorado, B.S.
Alliance Francaise, Paris
Harrington Institute of Interior Design

PUBLISHED IN:
Interior Design
Better Homes & Gardens
Professional Builder
Chicago Tribune
Designers West
Barron's Who's Who in Interior Design
Chicago Sun Times
Electricity
Pioneer Press
Colorado Homes & Lifestyles
Interiors & Sources
Southern Accents

PHILOSOPHY:
Our efforts focus on a forward thinking attitude and diversity in design styles which meet the individuality and aesthetic tastes of our clients. Our design enhances the established architecture with appropriateness of materials and details. Our interior design creates timeless, beautiful, and very special residences and public spaces. We strive in all aspects for the best, and offer a close working relationship, integrity and superior service.

SARA ZOOK
DESIGNS, LTD.

ABOVE: A brick barrel-vaulted ceiling and lighted coves bring warmth and casualness, while richly colored antiques and wool damask drapes add to the sense of comfort. The iron and crystal chandelier brings together the formal chairs with the informal brick.

RIGHT: The rich colors of an antique Oriental rug set the mood for this library detailed in warm cherry. The coffered ceiling is backlit around the cove to enhance comfort and coziness, while upholstered shutters in an Oriental chintz add softness.

ABOVE: A 1970s house with dark pine post-and-beam construction, rough cedar and moss rock was renovated into an airy contemporary expansive residence highlighting expansive views of the mountains in Snowmass, Colorado. Evening sunsets cast blue and purple hues, inspiring the use of rich jewel tones against a light background.

LEFT: Original 4x4 posts were sheathed in drywall to form large columns and connected with a glass wall in the dining room to enhance privacy. The contemporary Navajo weaving above the fireplace adds to the regional uniqueness of the space.

INDEX
OF
INTERIOR
DESIGNERS

BELOW: Ron Wilson Designer: A black lacquer dining group introduces a dash of sleek contemporary living to an area that otherwise emphasizes natural materials and greenery.

INDEX
OF
PHOTOGRAPHERS

OPPOSITE: Edward C. Turrentine
Interior Design, Inc.
The atrium commands attention,
while classic furnishings and exotic accessories
add the flavor of faraway lands.